THE QUILTING PATH

A GUIDE TO SPIRITUAL DISCOVERY THROUGH FABRIC, THREAD AND KABBALAH

LOUISE SILK

Walking Together, Finding the Way®
SKYLIGHT PATHS®
PUBLISHING
Woodstock, Vermont

www.skylightpaths.com

The Quilting Path:
A Guide to Spiritual Discovery through Fabric, Thread and Kabbalah

2006 First Printing
© 2006 by Louise Silk

For information regarding permission to reprint material from this book, please write or fax your request to SkyLight Paths Publishing, Permissions Department, at the address / fax number listed below, or e-mail your request to permissions@skylightpaths.com.

Grateful acknowledgment is given for permission to reprint material from the following sources:
Photographs © 2006 by Peter Shefler, Clearstory Studios. Visit http://www.healing-arts.org/clearstory.
Illustrations © 2006 by Sarah Silk
SilkQuilt.com by Eli Silk

Library of Congress Cataloging-in-Publication Data

Silk, Louise.
The quilting path : a guide to spiritual discovery through fabric, thread, and Kabbalah / Louise Silk.
p. cm.
ISBN-13: 978-1-59473-206-5 (pbk.)
ISBN-10: 1-59473-206-X (pbk.)
1. Quilting—Patterns. 2. Patchwork—Patterns. I. Title.

TT835.S515 2006
746.46—dc22

2006016530

10 9 8 7 6 5 4 3 2 1

Manufactured in Canada
Cover Design: Sara Dismukes

SkyLight Paths Publishing is creating a place where people of different spiritual traditions come together for challenge and inspiration, a place where we can help each other understand the mystery that lies at the heart of our existence.

SkyLight Paths sees both believers and seekers as a community that increasingly transcends traditional boundaries of religion and denomination—people wanting to learn from each other, *walking together, finding the way.*

SkyLight Paths, "Walking Together, Finding the Way," and colophon are trademarks of LongHill Partners, Inc., registered in the U.S. Patent and Trademark Office.

Walking Together, Finding the Way®
Published by SkyLight Paths Publishing
A Division of LongHill Partners, Inc.
Sunset Farm Offices, Route 4, P.O. Box 237
Woodstock, VT 05091
Tel: (802) 457-4000   Fax: (802) 457-4004
www.skylightpaths.com

With deepest gratitude to my children

CONTENTS

CONTENTS

Preface

I WAS THERE, NOW I AM HERE

I am a quilting mystic born into a Jewish culture following a Buddhist practice. Making literal sense of the description is far more difficult than being and doing my life moment to moment. Living and working in a large airy loft in an urban setting allows me the expansive luxury of fitting seemingly disparate things together in a perfect patchwork blending of matter and spirit.

My longing for intimate communion with the Divine showed itself in my childhood. My parents were Zionists believing in and working tirelessly for the Jewish State of Israel, but I never saw Friday night candles or any form of prayer. Still, my dad would often tease me that if I weren't careful, I could end up the perfect *rebbitzin*. A *rebbitzin* is the wife of a rabbi. In his view, that was the best possibility for an observant woman, and at that time that might have been the way it actually worked. That was his authentication of my spiritual leanings.

My religious quest picked up its pace after I had children. They had questions, but I didn't have answers. Why do the holidays begin at sundown? Why are people constantly getting up and sitting down in the synagogue service? I seized the opportunity to join with other women in an adult bat mitzvah class and finally mastered the basics. A bat mitzvah is a ritual in which a twelve-year-old girl demonstrates her religious knowledge and in doing so agrees to become an adult member of the community. Being thirty-five years old instead of twelve made all the difference for me. I loved the learning and longed to know more.

At that point in my life, I had already established myself as a professional quilt maker and had made a concerted effort to keep my religion separate from my work. In my experience, quilters were not Jewish, and Jews did not quilt. I was not going to buck the system and be the first attempting to mix them together.

Then one day I had a revelation. I was driving home from a meeting where I was coordinating a volunteer effort to resettle Soviet Jews in Pittsburgh. I knew and understood quite suddenly that my quilting needed the content of my Jewish experience to grow.

I began on a path of serious religious study, processing and expressing the information through the movement of needle and thread. I gathered knowledge by reading, participating in study and meditation groups, and attending adult educational and retreat centers. Throughout each experience, I processed the information by expressing it visually in cloth. My quilts took shape as wall hangings, books, calendars, garments, and even a tent. I finally understood my learning style: integration of knowledge through my affinity for fiber.

It works for me, and it is my gift to you: a practical quilting guide on the path of simple oneness. It is my unmitigated joy to share the fortune. Be one with me, one with others on the path, and one with the quilts.

Following Your Bliss

Every summer I spend a week vacationing with a dear friend. She is a devoted Catholic who believes very strongly in all the religious tenets and traditions. When I ask her what religion offers, she rattles off a succinct list: tradition, culture, history, prayer, meditation, ritual, community, taking care of one's self, creation, and the larger self-connection to a Godhead.

Every religion has symbols for the sacredness that bring us comfort, understanding, and an opening into spirit. Because of my personal experience, I most often relate to images associated with Jewish mysticism and Zen Buddhism. Symbols are a means to the sacred. Our job is to put ourselves right smack in the middle of whatever we choose. For this book, we will use the mystical tree of life. We will put ourselves into the thick of it, and it will manifest within us.

As each encompasses the other, we will discover that we are always in sacred time and in all ways with divinity. We are unique individuals in the similar situation of sacredness.

Life's work is to wake up. The only way is to be open, to be curious, and to develop some sense of empathy and sympathy for everything that comes our way. We are obligated to know life's nature, and let it teach us what it will. We really have no choice. If we don't flow with and accept the lessons, they will keep coming to us. We can try to run away, to manipulate our world to make it look smooth, but the angels and demons will keep appearing until we heed the lessons and turn the corner. The choice is ours. We have the power to choose. We are given everything we need. It's all within us: happiness and joy, pain and sorrow. Acceptance is our vehicle of liberation, and joy is celebrating quilt making in our lives. Bliss is the warmth of batting, the texture of cloth, and the tactile nature of the stitch.

My quilting has always been my spiritual practice, but it took me years to comprehend that as my truth. Before I began my religious studies, the first hint came when I understood that the process of making a quilt is more important to me than the quilt product. How did I figure that out? After I finished a piece I would find myself in a deep depression. I had lost my pleasure and it made me sad. I feared I would never again experience the euphoria I felt creating the quilt. Then I would begin the next quilt, and to my amazement I experienced the same lifting of spirit and renewal of life's purpose. To maintain my exultant state, I developed a system of working on one piece while allowing two or three more to form in my mind. The process of planning, creating, completing, and starting anew was the key to my happiness.

I did not come out of a quilting tradition. No one in my family made quilts. Still, from my very first quilt onward, I experienced how quilts adapted to suit me. The whole process was both adapting and adaptive. Quilts and I formed each other. Having experienced this firsthand, I'm convinced it's a possibility for anyone.

Quilt making is easy to learn. There was a time in our history when every family had several quilt makers. Quilts rested on every bed, table, and chair. Some were for everyday use; others memorialized special occasions and relationships. Women passed their skills on to their children, and experienced quilt makers were considered valuable assets to everyday community life. Those who didn't create the quilts with their own hands still were knowledgeable about quilting materials and the process. Although industrialization has lured us away from this home-centered activity, it does not eliminate our capability to learn the craft. As our potential for quilt appreciation reveals itself, this book provides the information and direct instruction necessary to transform pieces of dreams into patchwork realities.

For whom is this book written? Really, it's for everyone, old and young, male and female, novice and expert, rich and poor. Basic needlework skills are not even necessary. You only need the willingness to learn about patchwork quilting and its spiritual life connections.

This is a hands-on book. Bring to it an openhearted acceptance, looking at each moment as a thing in itself in wholeness and completeness. I hope you will enjoy my personal anecdotes, but I tell them only to encourage you to take on the experiences for yourself. It's time to press the refresh button and look beyond the personal. Nurture the flow of change, stitch by stitch, as you appreciate the fruits of your labor, while kindling a value and appreciation of handwork.

I have a good friend who never reads a book straight through from beginning to end. For her, a page somewhere in the middle is always the right place to start. Like reading a book of short stories or a basic craft project book, you may not want to start at the first chapter. Begin by reading the introduction, which contains all the basic information. Then go where you are drawn. Chapter 1, for instance, presents a project that is not simple for a beginner. At the same time, it's a practical quilt that everyone loves and wants to make a dozen times over. You may find you can go right to it, or you may need to build more basic skills. Each project has several variations so that you can adapt it to suit you and build your confidence and increase your knowledge.

Most of us don't try new things out of fear of failure. The only failure here would be *not* to make the attempt. You have everything you need. Fear is a distraction. Be diligent with your attention, your questions, and your sincerity, and all will be revealed.

Quilts as Metaphor

What is a quilt? By definition, a quilt has three layers of material joined together by hand or machine stitching. The top layer is an intricate composition of different fabrics and patterns. The interior is a chaos of multiple threads, fibers, and knots. On the back, a gathering of hundreds upon hundreds of stitch indentations is displayed, a proud testament to the work of the quilter. The patchwork quilt is a spectacular format.

This repository of textures has many uses in addition to the traditional bed cover. A quilt or a quilted piece can adorn the body or be displayed as a wall decoration. Today, there is a vibrant art-quilt movement. Quilts as works of art are displayed in galleries and private settings, providing moments of wonder and astonishment.

Painstakingly cut, pieced, and sewn, the making of a quilt moves in slow motion in contrast to the rest of the world, which reels ahead on fast-forward. Quilts may seem anachronistic in today's speedy computer-focused world, but that is not so. The quilting process remains as useful today as it did in the time of our ancestors. While we grapple with expanding technological boundaries and frontiers, the quilter still uses needle and thread to hold together pieces, fragments, and parts that would otherwise remain scattered and disparate. This attention to detail is precisely the source of a quilt's value, offering a practice that gives us a completely whole look at our place in the universe no matter which way we turn. There is no need to go far. There is pure delight in the fiber we find on us and all around us.

A patchwork quilt is a hands-on art form, but it is also useful as a life metaphor. Its versatile mixture of colors, textures, and shapes, when stitched together, can represent just about anything. Quilting is a process just as life is a process. Quilts are a sum of many pieces joined together, just as life is a sum of time and experience. Each quilt, while being individual and unique, employs multiple variations on continually repeating patterns. Life is much the same with endless variations on repeating themes coming together as the summation of a lifetime.

This book is an opportunity to acquire skill, insight, experience, and mystery. Skill is acquired by diligence. Insight comes to us by gift from the universe. The mystery occurs in a flash when at some point during the quilting journey, the combination of eyes, fingers, needle, thread, fabric, artistic inspiration, and heartbeat all gather to create the experience, and we realize that we'll never really know how it's done. When mystery is met, gratitude follows.

While you engage in the creative process of fashioning a series of quilts, I invite you to apply the quilting metaphor to your particular life experience. You will joyfully stimulate your creative center; discover an American craft form with a proud cultural tradition; and rise above that which threatens to flatten life. Experience a life view that is passionate, creative, humorous, and artful. Luxuriate in the richness of fragment and totality, durability and aging, vibrancy and fading. Everything that you invest into creating a quilt will escalate your personal growth and exploration, and your quilt product will remain forever to tickle your memory with a treasure of associations.

Introduction
THREADING THE BASICS

One day in the 1990s I was having lunch with my aging mom and dad. I was quite animated as I explained the discoveries of a current quilting project. My mom was in the advanced stages of Alzheimer's disease. She looked over at me inquisitively and innocently asked, "Where did you come from?" It was clear I fascinated her, and she was trying to figure out how she and I fit together. Then she added, "I really wish your nana could see you now. She always thought you were cute and stupid."

I was dumbfounded and blankly stared back at her. Then the thought entered my mind that maybe my blank look was part of the reason Nana thought I was stupid. I produced one of my classic grimaces, added a nervous giggle, and began sharing more about my quilt-making tale, ignoring both Mom's question and her comment.

Why do I share this little story? To show you that we all have limits placed upon us by our past. We come out of the womb, newborn, and then we are bombarded with one thing after another. There is always something. Some are benign and harmless, but too many are malignant, ugly, hurtful, and limiting. My mom's statement made me realize what I'd been struggling with all of my life. Not only did my nana think I was cute and stupid, my mom also thought I was cute and stupid. That's part of the source of my early childhood wounding. Understanding this brought the pieces and struggles of my life into focus.

It's quite a challenge to prove yourself to your mother. It becomes the work of a lifetime. Each and every one of us has it in some form. No one is exempt. It's part of the human process. Each of us has a history, a family, and some life situation we are striving to overcome—and that's part of why we do spiritual work. It helps us to discover, accept, and go beyond the limits placed upon us by others. At the same time this spiritual work provides direct understanding of our place in the divine plan.

I live my quilting. It is my practice. I work at it every single day. I might not always make it to my worktable, but I see a shirt, smell a flower, taste a food, and somehow, in some way, it relates to quilts. It's constant, but I haven't always been aware of or understood it. In fact, most of my life I struggled to hide this addiction to fiber. I wanted to fit in and be liked, and I saw my love of fiber as an obsession that limited people's ability to love me. I was wrong. My love of fiber is the truly authentic me, and as I grow into and accept the true me, I open to the miraculous consistent nature of the universe, the interconnectedness of all, and my rightful place within it. That's the practice—the acceptance of who we are and how to be and do our true selves. It is a practice, a process of living and life, that takes hours, days, weeks, months, and years—lots and lots of practice.

Anything can be a spiritual practice—really anything. If you love fiber and have a sense of its boundless possibilities, these techniques are for you. What better way to build a spiritual practice than doing what you love to do, being one with fabrics? Your love of fiber will help you along the spiritual path.

Being born a Jew, I always longed for a place in the religion that would satisfy my spiritual longing. That never happened for me within the formal institution. I would participate in a traditional ritual such as lighting Sabbath candles or attending a High Holiday Service and feel disappointment that I wasn't uplifted. I would attend some Jewish event and walk away with the severe self-criticism that it was my monkey-mind (as Buddhists call our distracting, chattering thoughts) that prevented me from making heavenly connections. I spent years and years trying every variation and location available, desperately searching for that "right" connection.

The place within the tradition where I finally found my relationship to and faith in the Divine is in the mystical philosophy called Kabbalah. Kabbalah is a spiritual communication system that helps us understand where we come from and why we are here on earth. From the beginning of time, mystics sought the answers to the true nature of creation and through Kabbalah were able to develop an applied system to divine connection. Kabbalah means to receive. It is the receiving from the source of all. Kabbalah is not a religion, and it is not just for Jews. It is for any seeker of any religious persuasion who can make use of it.

Kabbalah engages us as practitioners in a contemplative system that explains how this universe was created. Through a series of worlds or realms and a set of divine attributes, we come to understand a larger view of ourselves as humans created in the image of an all-knowing higher power. We come to understand and accept that we have within us each of the divine qualities combined with our human free will to integrate the Divine into our lives as we choose.

Because we were made in the likeness of the Divine, our spiritual practice affords us the opportunity to realize what life is, who we truly are, and what tasks the Divine wants us to perform. We need to have the patient open acceptance of a detached observer each and every day, then we are free to witness the multitudes of life experience. With this skill, we realize our authentic nature, seeing life simply as it is in all its wonder. Most religions agree on the oneness of our moment-to-moment being. In this book, the love of quilting is used as a training ground for integration. Each chapter is dedicated to a divine attribute. Tackling the quilting projects designed with a particular attribute in mind will help you experience these attributes personally in your life.

The Four Worlds of Kabbalah

Nearly all religions have a mystical segment, a means for us to have direct intimate contact with the Divine. Mystical or contemplative spirituality is an ever-deepening, personal relationship with our higher power. To the mystic, true contemplation is a gift of grace and delight from the beloved that takes us into new realms of understanding. The human need for satisfaction of the mind and emotions is always a part of our nature. The mystic goes beyond mind to deal with pure spirit, unfathomable intellect, and perfection beyond human grasp.

According to the Jewish mystical tradition, the purpose of creation is to provide the Divine with a dwelling place in the lower realms. The universe is created out of nothingness from a single point of light. The nothingness is called *Ain Sof*. It is the infinite absolute, the Divine that is beyond existence. For the Divine to exist outside of nothingness, the Divine created the universe in a system of progressively denser and more physical worlds. The worlds are said to serve as garments for divine light. A garment conceals the true nature of divinity so that a small part of it may be revealed to us.

According to Kabbalah, we live in a five-dimensional universe with four different worlds, ten directions, ten attributes, and thirty-two paths that constitute the totality of existence. The relationship between the physical and the spiritual is always dynamic. The Divine is acting in the earth through us, depending on us to work seamlessly in the world.

The first six dimensions of our universe are north, south, east, west, up, and down. This is the three-dimensional physical world with which we are most familiar. The seventh and eighth dimensions are time and space, which encompass the past, present, and future. In this dimension, shape-shifting and shifts in space and time occur. We might think of this as a kind of magic, but it's more about the inner connectedness of all things. The ninth and tenth dimensions are the spirit or soul dimensions of good and evil.

The constriction or the covering of *Ain Sof* with garments sets the stage for humans to freely elect to work with the Divine, choosing light over darkness and good over evil. The very existence of evil is solely for our benefit so that we will transform the evil by the act of choosing goodness.

The four worlds represent the oscillation and conversion of energy into matter. The first world is called *Asiyah,* the world of activity or making. This is our physical world; the one of greatest intensity and definition and the closest to our everyday notion of reality, behavior, and action. In it, time is linear and our five senses are our basic mode for perception and survival. Because events occur sequentially, we can fall into habit and repetition. This becomes a barrier to our perception of the inner nature of divinity. Heaven is not here on earth; it is up in the sky.

In *Asiyah* the ego, our personality, is highly differentiated from the other and constantly refers back to self, keeping our spirit side in deep shadow. We are not aware of the inner self or consciousness, and we do not question right action. In this tribal state, religion equals ritual and behaviorism gives rise to magic. In my story, *Asiyah* shows itself as my parents and I meeting our basic physical needs of sustenance over lunch in a pleasant social environment.

The second world is *Yetzeriah,* the world of formation. This is the realm of angels and spiritual forces immediately beyond our physical domain. Here we find archetypes and myths, such as the hero's journey. In *Yetzeriah,* we form thoughts and feelings; these thought forms are precursors to acting creatively in the world.

In this world our wounded ego is the vehicle on our journey to the Divine. Being able to see beyond the self, we explore our relationship to pain and suffering in the intermediate state on the path toward awakening. We live our story in the past with separateness as a psychological self-seeking control of the journey. Here time is bi-directional, going from past to present to future and back again. Applying the world of formation to my lunch with my mother, we see the psychological pain of a daughter longing for the love of a mother.

The third world is *Briyah,* the world of creation. In this soul universe, we have an intimate awareness of the Divine, yet at the same time accept separation. Memory operates in the now, in holographic time, where one moment is both itself and many other moments and subject and object are one. We are able to hold opposites as we understand ourselves as individuals included in something larger.

In the world of creation, I am no longer fixed in my story. I understand and accept that I am a daughter continually searching for love from my mother, and at the very same time I am no longer dependent on my mother's love to participate in the universe as a creative quilt maker.

The fourth and final world is *Atzilut,* the world of emanation, translated as "nothingness." This world is in such close proximity to *Ain Sof* that it is fully absorbed in the Divine. *Atzilut* is difficult to describe because this level of reality cannot be known to humans. This world is the domain of the *sefirot,* the divine attributes used to create and oversee the universe. Here they are undifferentiated. We need the lower universes to conceive them as separate forces.

The Tree of Life and the Divine Attributes

To apply Kabbalah to our quilting, we must take a little time to understand how it operates. *Sefirot,* the ten divine attributes, are the most basic mode of the Divine's creative power (see the *sefirot* diagram on p. 18). Constituting the inner structure and makeup of the universes described in the Kabbalah, these attributes permit us to speak about divine creation without actually defining it. The s*efirot* are delineating, limiting lights that serve as the bridge to reveal and express divine greatness in our finite realm. This makes it possible for an infinite and transcendental Godhead to interact with us as part of the creation. Saying that humans are made "in the image of God" means they are a microcosm of the Divine's creative powers. Through the *sefirot,* the Divine limits its infinite essence and manifests specific qualities that we, the creation, can grasp and relate to as a place to begin understanding our divine relationship. The basic concepts of the *sefirot* come into existence in *Atzilut* and become more and more manifest as they go further into the worlds. Each universe contains all the *sefirot.*

The highest faculty in humans is free will, through which we decide how we will think, feel, and act as we rise above all internal pressures or external circumstances. This will corresponds to the highest of the ten *sefirot—keter,* meaning crown. This level of our transcendental nature precedes creative activity. We are united with the Divine's will and desire to create a world for us.

Keter is the uppermost aspect of the tree of life and the first in the path to mystical consciousness. No human can truly attain its essence. It's enough to know that this is where we begin. Going forward, we will look at each of the attributes on the tree and apply them to our quilting practice.

Spirituality and religion are separate elements. Religion enforces an external institutionalized system of attitudes, beliefs, and practices. Mysticism or spirituality is an internal search, directing our mind to our heart. The Divine is not something external waiting to punish us for our transgressions. It is inside us enduring our punishment with us. Spirituality focuses our attention on the divine grace radiating from our own hearts. Our spirituality brings us to focus the mind inward and approach ourselves with love. We see the Divine from within as an altered light that is always accessible and easily reachable.

To begin any practice, whether quilting or contemplation, we cultivate our personal and intimate path. We cannot examine it from a distance as if it belongs to someone else. We walk it for ourselves. We invest ourselves in our practice, knowing that nothing happens by magic. We agree to a working system that will give the desired results.

From personal experience, I believe that all practices begin with meditation. Meditation teaches us focus. As we get more focused, we will apply our meditation experience to our quilting, but it's easiest to start with simple meditation.

We are always doing things to cover up our basic existential anxiety. This builds a conditioned view of life. Our practice is to wake up to life as it is without having to achieve something, to simply be with what is. Meditation is done with complete effort and total attention; when the mind drifts, the meditation brings it back to the point of attention, such as the breath or a mantra. The work is paying attention and taking care of what needs to be done right in that moment. In Sanskrit, it is called *samadhi,* total oneness with the object.

We make a moment-to-moment choice between the world we set up in our heads and what really is. Our faith helps us to do the practice: sitting every day and going through the confusion. Be patient and respect yourself for doing the practice. The practice enables you to face yourself. Trust and acceptance in things being as they are is the secret of life. When we truly open up to our lives as they are, we open to all life.

Meditation and the Quilting Path

Observe the breath going in and out. You don't need to make it special, simply be aware of your breathing, one breath at a time. Your mind wanders: it doesn't matter; don't judge or analyze it. Gently let go and return your attention to your breathing. This act of beginning again is the essential art of meditation practice, and it happens over and over again.

If you feel yourself getting sleepy, try sitting a bit straighter. If your eyes are closed, open them slightly. Take a few deep conscious breaths before returning to simply observing.

To cultivate a daily practice:

- Plan to meditate at the same time every day.
- Establish a meditation space where you will not be disturbed.
- Gather inspirational objects in your space: flowers, images, tokens, incense.

- Determine before you begin how long you will sit and use a timer. Even five minutes will help you cultivate and maintain your awareness throughout the day.
- Find a comfortable posture with a straight back. Do not move at all during the meditation.

Kabbalah uses the term *garments* when speaking of the nature of ordinary reality. In meditation or prayer, the mind is able to pass through its own garments into the higher worlds of consciousness. The higher or deeper one reaches, the more subtle and diaphanous the spiritual barriers become. There is more light and less form, until a level is reached where the light is stronger than the mind.

It is easy to feel resistance or fear as you begin this process. Adopt a friendly, patient attitude toward yourself. It takes time to let go of control, which is symptomatic of our constant striving for more or something better. It's not called a process and a practice without good reason. Eventually you will transfer what you develop in your meditation practice to your quilting practice. In that way, you will use the quilting process to experience the Divine.

General Quilting Instructions

This section contains the basic information you will need to begin making quilts. Volumes have been written on quilting techniques. Don't get bogged down in that minutiae. Over time, you will develop your own style and skill. Read over all the information that follows before getting started. Some of it will be difficult to understand, but once you get started, it will make more sense.

Design

The most successful patchwork uses a variety of light, medium, and dark values, regardless of hue. It doesn't matter what color scheme you choose—that is a personal, aesthetic decision.

- Use a variety of lights, mediums, and darks in any hue you like.

- Select a variety of prints and textures to create visual interest.

- Trust your senses, your feelings, and your intuition!

Color

In the world of artists and quilters, color is called hue. The primary hues are red, blue, and yellow. The secondary hues are purple, green, and orange. When we mix all three primaries together we get brown. When we mix complementary colors together, such as red and green, blue and orange, or yellow and purple, we get gray. These primary and secondary colors are often shown on a color wheel. Then it is easy to see analogous colors, colors next to each other on the wheel, and complementary colors, colors opposite to each other on the wheel. If we add white to a color we make a tint, and if we add black, we make a shade. This can be done in whatever way color is added to the fabric, usually with dye.

There are absolutely no secrets about color. Use what you like and what you are drawn to. Trust your feelings. They will serve you well. Really, anything goes in combining color for quilts. I always point to the traditional Amish quilts that work beautifully with so many unthinkable combinations of color. Color is visual joy, the ultimate in eye candy. Be brave, this is a great exploration opportunity.

Fabrics

When you go to one of your local chain fabric stores, you will encounter quilting departments that contain a sea of medium-value small-scale prints. Most fabric buyers do not do piece work, and they don't understand the importance of value and scale. But now you do, so it is your job to hunt around for the full range of value and scale and use it on every project.

This is a good reason to support your local quilt shops. You will find them listed in the yellow pages under quilting supplies. These women and men work hard to give great service and supply an impressive inventory. They are quilters who understand the love and joy of patchwork. They need a loyal customer, you, to stay in business. Please tell them I sent you!

In the beginning, keep your purchases to a minimum. Your tastes will change as your knowledge and experience grow. Expect to make many trips to the fabric store— that's part of the pleasure. The first time you go, allow a minimum of two hours.

First, survey the bolts of fabric and see what draws you, such as a particular color, pattern, or texture. Next, head over to the notions section to check out the products. Don't be afraid to ask questions if you don't know what something is. Finally, look through the quilt-making books and survey potential patchwork projects. This warm-up should be relaxing and enjoyable.

Always buy the best materials you can afford. A quilt can last more than a lifetime and will require lots of hard work and hours of labor. Don't waste your time with misplaced thrift.

For most of the projects, particularly until you get more experience, use 100 percent cotton fabric. It has a great feel, softens with age, and holds folds when pressed that make it the easiest material to use. Quilter's cotton is preshrunk and resistant to bleeding and does not need to be washed before using. Today, there are many companies making fabrics specifically for use in patchwork. Seek them out—they will help you with color and design selection.

The exception to this will be when you are using recycled materials. When you are using items of clothing and textiles that you associate with something in your past, you must figure out how to use it in a meaningful way despite the restrictions in color, texture, and design. If you have limited experience, successfully complete several projects with new fabrics and gain some confidence before using recycled materials.

When it is time to select the materials and supplies for your first project, bring this book and work directly from the supply list for that project. First select a color you like, and then find a fabric in that hue that particularly attracts you. Remove the bolt of cloth from the shelf and match it to other fabrics that interest you. Keep in mind the design rules: selecting a variety of shades and textures. You will now begin a long process of adding and subtracting fabric bolts until you come up with the perfect mix.

I often use thrift shops as a source for alternative materials. I plan my trips for the half-price days. I look for big garments that can provide a large amount of material. Choose items that have varying textures but are on the heavier side so they are easy to sew and offer interesting applications and closures. Wherever you get your materials, take your time, relax, and have fun!

Equipment

For piecing, a simple straight stitch portable sewing machine is all you need. If you don't own one, start to ask around. You may find a family member or friend who has an old unused machine gathering dust. Take it to your local fabric store when a technician is present and have him or her adjust the tension, clean it, and teach you how to thread it properly and replace a needle. That's all you need to do for any of the machine-stitched projects included here.

I know some of you are shaking your head right now and saying you intend to do all of your work by hand, so you won't need a sewing machine. Yes, if you prefer, you can do any of the projects in this book with hand stitching. However, my experience is that even those students who insist on handwork soon become impatient with the slow progress of their piecework once they observe their friends quickly finishing project after project.

I myself love handwork more than anything else I do in the needlecrafts, but there is a time and a place for it. The best use of handwork is in hand quilting, attaching patchwork top to a batting and a backing, but the most effective way to make patchwork is by machine. I will advise you on each project when to make the best use of both hand and machine techniques. You will be handicapped if you don't get a machine and learn to use it.

A rotary cutter, mat, and plastic ruler are essential. Buy the biggest cutter and ruler that feel comfortable in your hand and the biggest mat you can afford that fits on your worktable. Fabric stores always put these items on sale—the loss leaders that bring us into their stores. Check the newspaper or call and ask to be put on the mailing list.

Using a cutting board.

You will also need a good pair of sewing shears, smaller thread clippers, and scissors for cutting paper. The blades of fabric shears are dulled if used to cut paper.

A steam iron is essential. Find the lightest one with the biggest soleplate. Check *Consumer Reports* and go with their highest recommendation.

For machine sewing, any kind of sewing thread works well. For handwork, use quilting thread. It has a silicon finish that keeps it from knotting while you work.

Quilting needles are called "betweens." They are shorter than embroidery or hand-sewing needles, and are numbered by size— the higher the number, the smaller the needle. Start with a mixed pack of sizes 5 to 10 and see what feels comfortable.

Pins, a seam ripper, a see-through ruler, plastic for making templates, a mechanical pencil, a tape measure, and $1/4$-inch graph paper are the other essential notions, all readily available at fabric stores.

Work Space

Find a corner you can call your own. It is imperative to have a place for your machine and not have to put it away at the end of each session. Students tell me this is one of my best pieces of advice. Part of saying that this activity is important to both you and your family is allowing it to have the space it deserves!

As you purchase fabrics for a specific project, keep them together. Leftover fabrics or the fabrics you buy to build a collection are best arranged by color.

Set up near the biggest worktable available.

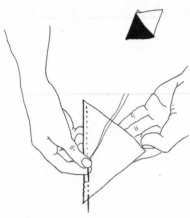

Hand piecing.

Chain piecing.

Patchwork Construction

All seams in patchwork are $1/4$-inch, whereas clothing uses a $5/8$-inch seam. This is a warning: Patchwork is not sewing; it has its own set of rules. Do not think that any of your sewing rules apply here; it will just be a source of frustration.

All measurements given in this book are finished dimensions, that is, what the piece will measure after it has been sewn into the patchwork. When you are cutting a piece from the directions in the book, you must make sure the $1/4$-inch seam allowance is included; if it isn't, add it before cutting.

For hand piecing, use a single piece of quilting thread. Start and end $1/4$ inch from the cut edge and stitch along the $1/4$-inch seam line. Make a small running stitch putting three or four stitches on the needle at a time. After each set of stitches, do a back stitch by starting slightly behind the last complete stitch. The back stitch helps secures the hand stitching.

For machine stitching, you do not always need to back stitch. If the row you are sewing will be overlapped by another row of stitching in the next step, do not take the time to back stitch. The second row of stitching will hold the first row of threads in place. If, however, there will not be an overlap, you must take the time to back stitch, which locks the threads in place.

Chain piecing is a wonderful machine technique that helps get the patchwork organized and sewn quickly and efficiently. The idea is to sew many sets of patches together without cutting the thread between each set. For example, if I wanted to take sets of two right triangles and turn them into squares, I would sit at my machine with piles of triangles, take two, line them up and sew them, and then continue right on to the next two triangles without lifting the presser foot or cutting the thread. You will end up with a long chain of the pieced triangles that can be cut apart, pressed and ready to use in the next step of the construction.

Be careful to match seams vertically and horizontally. It's okay to have some puckers (these go with the look of a quilt), but seams that don't meet will stick out and bother you.

Always press your work with the right side up. It does not matter which way the seams fall on the wrong side—to the right or to the left. It does matter how your piece looks from the front. There are only two important points about pressing.

First, don't use an iron that is too hot. Cotton is the hottest setting on most irons, and for the most part it's too hot. Stick to wool or the lowest setting that still uses steam. Steam is very important, more important than heat, which can scorch the fabric.

Second, you will be pressing, not ironing. Ironing is a back-and-forth motion with the iron. It stretches and pulls the fabric from its original grain and alters its shape. Instead, press, which is an up and down motion of the iron.

Quilt-as-You-Go Technique

In the quilt-as-you-go technique, you piece the fabrics and attach them to the backing and the batting, all in one step. I use this technique a lot. It makes it possible to complete a project in half the time and still get the great look of complicated patchwork. It eliminates the quilting stitch on the surface of the quilt, because each piece of patchwork is sewn to the batting and the background as it is sewn to its adjoining fabric patch.

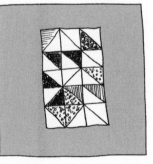

Quilt-as-you-go.

Finishing the Quilt

To bind the quilt, trim the batting and the backing even with the pieced top of the quilt. Cut 2½-inch-wide straight-grain strips from the leftovers of the project. Piece these together on the 2½-inch edge until there is enough to go around the perimeter of the quilt. Fold the strip in half lengthwise, wrong side together. Stitch to the wrong side of the quilt, going through all three layers. Leave the needle in at each corner, turning the quilt to make a right angle. Overlap the beginning and the end of the binding. Turn to the front and hand or machine stitch to the front, easing in at the corners.

If you want to hang the finished quilt, you will need a sleeve on the back at the upper edge, through which you can insert a rod or hanger. To prepare a sleeve, cut a 10-inch-wide strip the length of the top of the quilt. Turn under and stitch the short edges ½ inch; press in half, right side out. You can stitch these raw edges in at the top when you apply the binding, and then hand stitch the bottom fold to the back of the quilt as the last step.

Sign and date your quilt on the front or the back. You can use embroidery or a permanent ink marker.

Pillow Finishing Technique

1. Complete the pillow top. Trim the batting and backing to match the edges of the pillow top.

2. Cut the backing the width of the pillow top and 6–8 inches longer than its length. Take this piece and cut it into two, one piece being one-third of the length and the other being two-thirds.

3. Turn under ¼-inch along the cut edge and machine stitch to create a finished edge. Use the selvage edge of the second piece as the finished edge. Turn under and press a 1-inch hem in place on the larger piece.

4. Lay this piece on the front of the pillow top, right sides together. Cover the pillow top with the other piece, arranging the finished edge over the 1-inch hem.

5. Stitch along the perimeter of the pillow through all layers, maintaining the folded hem in the first backing piece and overlap the smaller piece over the larger hemmed backing piece.

6. Trim the corners diagonally to remove excess corner fabric. Turn the pillow right side out through the opening in the backing. Press. Slip the pillow form into the back opening.

If you are interested in making an alternative pillow backing, try using the front of a man's woven shirt as the back of the pillow. This method is explained in chapter 3. The button placket opening becomes the pillow opening on the back.

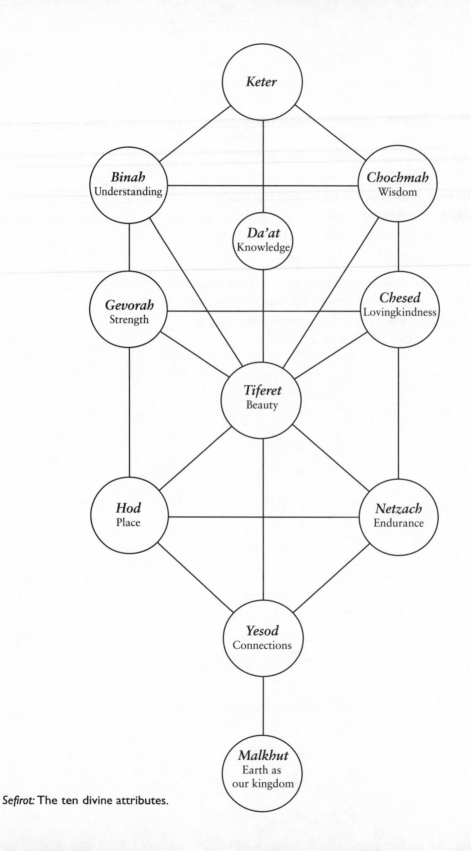

Sefirot: The ten divine attributes.

IT IS WHAT IT IS

One-Patch Utility Quilt

Chochmah: *the first conscious intellectual force in the creative process.*

Early on the Saturday morning after Thanksgiving, I made a run to the airport. My daughter was returning to her young adult life in Manhattan. The drive signaled the conclusion of an annual holiday and the beginning of my winter work season. I love to take people to and from the airport. It's a way to experience coming and going vicariously. There is such anticipation, excitement, and planning involved in the arrival, and an equal but opposite despair, sadness, and aimlessness after saying goodbye. Every hello guarantees a goodbye. That concept still makes my head shake in wonder because I'm your typical suffering human wanting to hurry beyond the awkward hellos and desperately avoiding the closing goodbyes.

Thanksgiving in the United States is a unique holiday because most Americans, regardless of religion, celebrate it. Growing up, I was one element of a large extended family. My mother served as the matriarch, always hosting the traditional turkey dinner at our home. We had it catered by a local caterer. The great tradition for me was to get up in the early morning and go to pick up the meal with my dad. Daddy would overindulge us by loading our basket with all kinds of rich and decadent foods, such as burnt pretzels, pigs-in-a-blanket, chocolates, mints, and special sodas. Along with three fifteen-pound turkeys, the caterer supplied us with all the trimmings: chestnut and plain bread stuffing, sweet potatoes, and lots and lots of gravy. On the way home, we would deposit one of the turkeys at my aunt's house. She and her family had Thanksgiving dinner with us, but she also got her own turkey so she would have the coveted leftovers to consume over the next week.

Being a family of retailers, this was our last chance to relax and be together before the holiday season kicked in. The next day and each day thereafter until Christmas, each of us would take our various stations at assorted cash registers throughout the area hoping for sales figures beating the year before. Thanksgiving was the last hurrah with drink, food, merriment, and football for the twenty or so family participants.

I've had to kiss those idyllic childhood Thanksgivings goodbye, one more proof that nothing lasts forever. The caterer closed, our retail business was sold, and family membership dwindled. I tried to revive the family gatherings in my home, adding new friends and discovering the secrets of roasting a turkey with all the trimmings. The final seal of Thanksgiving's fate occurred when my husband of twenty-three years chose that special day to tell our children he was moving out. This was the most significant ending of all.

I was married to my childhood sweetheart. I can clearly visualize the moment of our meeting. It was in ninth grade, hanging out one Friday night as part of a social group of boys and girls. He was cute, all decked out in his madras shirt, khaki pants, and Levi jacket. He walked in front of me but kept looking over his shoulder to make sure I was watching him. We were both smitten. It was love at first sight. Visualizing it now, I remember the feeling of that initial chemistry. Many years and three children later, we had a crisis that showed us we had lost our emotional bond. With that, he decided to move on to a different life and a fresh love.

By the beginning of the New Year, he was gone. I was destroyed. He was the only existence I knew, and I fervently believed my life was over without that youthful love bond. It felt like the worst thing that could and would ever happen to me. At the time even his death seemed a better option.

Then six weeks later, in February, standing by the stage door of a theater on Broadway, I met someone new. The exit of my childhood sweetheart allowed for the entrance of my spiritual soul mate. It was the unlikely union of a Canadian-born actor and a Pittsburgh-born quilt maker. He was the one who saw our couple potential. I had small vision. Having never been on a date, that was all I wanted. But once again there was a beginning, an initial interaction, a moment in time, where the heavens opened, all things were aligned and to quote him, "We locked eyeballs," and knew we were meant to be as one.

We had two years of bliss, experiencing life through each other's spirit. He introduced me to a Buddhist practice showing me its depth and breadth. I taught him the ethical value system underpinning Judaism. He encouraged the quilt maker in me, and I the actor in him. Then we found out he had a severe case of prostate cancer and a limited life span.

Heath had a way with words and he was very outspoken about the cancer. He didn't hesitate to share his feelings about the path. One of the most meaningful was his idea that cancer didn't happen to him, it happened for him. He used the illness to propel his spirit. I'm confident that as he made his grand exit he went on to join the bodhisattvas, those enlightened individuals who agree to return to earth until everyone is spiritually liberated.

Eight years after my sweetheart left I was once more experiencing an unalterable ending. Being grateful for my limited time with Heath, I began a fresh probation period accepting life without a partner. However, by this time I should have had enough life experience to know that when one door closes, another opens. This brings me to my current love. This perfectly unanticipated beginning was arranged through a good friend of mine who is his cousin. It turns out the last time she had seen him, she looked at him in a mirror and saw my image on top of his.

Our first meeting was halfway between our homes, which were some distance apart. We spent four hours together, and because it was the Fourth of July, we heard and saw fireworks around us. I knew the moment I saw him he was the one for me. I felt a physical draw—the right height, the exacting eyes, and the desirable arms. As we exchanged chronicles, the interconnected nature of our lives was uncanny—even his art forms in clay and photography use repeating patterns, similar to the format used in quilts. In the larger scheme, I had to come and go through two other partners to recognize and appreciate the special beauty of this new love.

Being One with Quilting

Think about one single day in your life. What about this very day? It is chock full of beginnings and endings, starts and stops, hellos and goodbyes. Going in and out of the bathroom, starting and ending a meal, and beginning and ending a telephone conversation are small examples. It is the nature of human life to be in a state of constant flux and change.

Beginnings and endings become even more pronounced as we apply the idea to our quilt making. First there is a separation problem. We think of ourselves and our quilts as two things. We have to stop our regular lives to pick up our quilting. We look at quilting as a leisure activity and one that only comes after the real work is completed. When we finally allow ourselves to begin the quilting process, we belabor each decision as if it is the beginning and the end of everything. We make the decisions so big that they become impossible to execute. Gradually, we build up a storehouse of unfinished projects because we don't know how to work our way through to the ending. When we do complete a project, we have a difficult time letting it go, let alone beginning something new.

Our work throughout the process of this book is to loosen up, become more fluid, have less separation and create a smoother circuit. Our goal is to be one with our quilting. It's exciting and at the same time difficult to figure out how to begin.

The *Chochmah* of the Unknown and Beyond

The divine attribute of *chochmah,* wisdom, is the "aha" moment. At the very instant we understand a quilting pattern, there are no words and there are no thoughts. There is only a split second of insight as we realize the possibility of a solution. This moment is soon followed by thought, and yet the moment itself is beyond or before thought. The flash of creativity that is *chochmah* is very close to the top of the Kabbalah tree of life where we find *keter,* nothingness. *Keter* is the moment before the twinkling, when the pattern is nothing because we don't yet know of it.

Chochmah stands as a passageway to *keter,* and as we move from one to the other, we trace the origin of our individual creative thought. It can be overwhelming to get an inkling of the multitude of our fortune. We tremble, shake, quiver, in the acknowledgment of wonder. Wisdom is the gateway to the awesomeness that lies beyond a thoughtless and formless world.

In its day-to-day form, the more wisdom expressed, the less we experience our egos, and the more selfless we become. As the intensity of our own ego diminishes, it is replaced by an acute awareness of the omnipresence of the Divine. *Chochmah* is the entry point for our creative capacity, and there is a *chochmah* point within each and every divine attribute.

Buddhists have a visual depiction of the worldly phenomena of the various states of being—impermanence, suffering, and no self—called the Wheel of Life and Death. We suffer because we imagine what is not really self to be part of us. We mix up that which is impermanent with that which is permanent.

Existence with these three characteristics is called *samsara*, which means we continually flow and move from one moment to the next and from one life to the next. *Samsara* is not the actual external world or life itself, but the way we interpret them. *Samsara* is life as we live it under the influence of ignorance, the subjective world each of us creates for

23

him- or herself. This world contains good and evil, joy and pain, happiness and sadness. These aspects are relative and not absolute. They can be defined only in relationship to each other and are continually changing along the spectrum of opposites. Although *samsara* seems to be all-powerful and all-pervading, it isn't. It is created by our own state of mind as in the world of a dream. It can be dissolved into nothingness just like awakening from a dream. We can awaken for a mere moment or for many moments in our lives. When we awaken to reality, even for a moment, the world does not disappear but is experienced in its true nature: pure, brilliant, sacred, and indestructible. The state of perfect enlightenment is deathless, unborn, and unchanging.

We think we understand the quilt pattern and we begin the process making it. We find we can't draw it correctly and must make adjustments. We search our fabric stash for the perfect complements and commit to them—only to discover we don't have enough of our favorite cloth. We carefully do our calculations, and then accidentally make the wrong cuts in the fabric. We can't get the machine to work properly, the thread keeps breaking, and in frustration, we put everything away.

The outer rim of the Buddhist Wheel of Life and Death is divided into twelve sections that are stages in the evolution of the individual being. The sections apply to our states of mind, which are continuously arising, developing, and passing away. We can trace back the causes of suffering to their root by means of these twelve sections or links in the chain of being, from the suffering of mortal life and death to its ultimate origin, ignorance. Doing this takes us to the development of the twelve stages: ignorance, conditioning, consciousness, name and form, the six senses, contact, sensation, thirst, grasping, existence, birth, and decay and death. The twelve links form an unending circle. At death we fall into a state of ignorance once more, and the cycle starts all over again. *Samsara* means going on and on, round and round, without beginning or end.

Our lives are shaped by our innermost thoughts and deepest motivations that occur on the most subtle and hidden level. These are most easily discovered through meditation techniques. We can use our artistic energy in quilt making as a link to our karmic force in the chain of being. Employing this energy, we continually create the world anew at each and every moment. In quilt making, we go through the full cycle of accepting our divinely inspired creativity, trusting that whatever happens is a gift, to thinking that, because we don't remember how to thread the sewing machine, we have no right to do this work.

We don't have to understand or believe in either Buddhism or Kabbalah to see that the general idea both in the Wheel of Life and Death and the divine attributes of the Tree of Life is that we are a very small piece of something quite large that is constantly moving and changing. Opportunities will appear over and over again. The love of quilts can be a portal to all that life has to offer.

Awareness, Intention, and Trust

It happens countless times a day, in every conceivable situation. We expect something to happen one way, and inevitably the result is not what we wanted or expected. How can we let go of the desired result? It is frustrating because whenever we assign a meaning or expectation to our actions, we are wrong. Attempting the quilt-making activities in this book is a letting go. While reading the information, you might find yourself resisting, thinking thoughts such as "This is too difficult to understand" or "This is all fine and good for her, the author, but it won't work for me, the reader." These mental blocks keep you on your particular wheel of *samsara*.

There is a personal solution to suffering. It is faith and trust. Faith becomes trust as it is lived; trust is active faith. Trusting the Divine means trusting life and living in the present. Living in the present, letting go of past and future, is an expression of our inner security with our use of *chochmah*. This ultimately depends on our faith in our place in a larger picture of meaning and immortality. By living in the present, everything is available at once. This awareness forces us deeper and deeper into the infinity of life and ultimate trust in the Divine.

Picture a devout woman praying. Her eyes are closed, her hands are clasped. She is swaying back and forth, her lips making barely perceptible movements. She is totally undistracted by her surroundings, and her entire being is focused on prayer. She is so deeply absorbed that she experiences each moment as the true and original moment. Imagine yourself spending the next hour stitching the pieces of your quilt. Could you bring that intense focus to your efforts? What would you learn? What new insights would you have? Would you be more successful tomorrow than you were yesterday?

The Hebrew word for this kind of concentration is *kavanah*. In the Jewish tradition *kavanah* is intention, an essential part of meaningful action. The term comes from the Hebrew root meaning to direct, intend, focus. The idea is to bring meaning to both the actions and the intention of those actions. Meaningful action is not something that happens haphazardly but rather is the confluence of a thoughtful decision about what we want to do coupled with the action of doing it.

One method of focusing our intention is ritual. Rituals and traditions mark specific times as holy, unique, and special. Rituals stop us at a point in time. They use the power of our history, language, and symbols to help us pause, take stock and pay attention to the moment. Ritual can function to direct our actions to hold, mark, celebrate, and fully experience time.

An example of a quilting ritual is the signing and dating of each piece at its completion. With the signature, all converges in one concentrated act intensifying the moment by linking us to something larger both vertically in time and horizontally in space. Through the signature, we travel in time connecting our names to past, present, and future and mark the moment with the essence of our history, people, family, tradition, values, and culture.

What's the difference between doing nothing that feels like wasting time and doing nothing that can feel wonderful and regenerating? Intention and ritual create holy moments that teach the importance of a time to be, to stop the action and appreciate the moment. With practices such as meditation, we become more observant of where we are right at every moment, and we begin to think of time differently.

When we go wandering in the fabric store or sit back and observe the progress of our work, we may or may not be living in the present. We are not in the moment if, in perusing the fabric bolts, we are thinking about all of our fabric wants. We are not in the moment if we are planning further goals and actions while we work on a current project. If we go into our past remembering previous actions and events or we go into the future thinking of deadlines and the consequences of not meeting them, it's likely we experience guilt. Our *kavanah*, our intention, is to be with what is, but because we haven't found a way to enter the present moment, our actions don't match our *kavanah*. Our task is to bring our intentions and our actions into sync.

In holy time we commit to living in a way where there is no past and no future, only the present. We create a moment-to-moment importance where everything is fine just as it is and we are good just the way we are. The key to intentionally creating an island in time is the advance commitment to set that time apart. With intention we change our relationship with time and stop trying to wrestle with it. Time stops being a burden and pressure. Time becomes a friend as we savor those precious chosen hours. Once we decide to set time apart for our work, we will fully experience living in the present. There is the added bonus: Living in the moment adds the power of that precious time shining through into other times, as each takes on its own significance and importance.

Another helpful approach is to differentiate process and product. While we will be working on the goal of making the project for each chapter, we will be better served concentrating on the how and why of our work. The product will be a

27

happy byproduct when we concentrate, use our *kavanah* and our rituals to simply show up and be with what is. Giving up emphasis on the product allows for more and greater potential with less unrealistic control over the results.

It is very possible to have a beginning panic and fear stepping into any process. To start something new is a risk, but recall the old adage, "Nothing ventured, nothing gained." Risk taking and even the fear associated with it are part of the creative process. They are there to push us over the edge. Life is short. Let's go at it with our bravery and our fears, no holds barred. Our fears have come out of past negative experiences. For many of us there is much negative experience with handwork. Maybe our past experiences were not successful. Maybe our standards were unrealistic. Maybe we're afraid we can't learn in this format. Maybe, maybe, and maybe. This is a brand new opportunity—seize it.

For faith to be alive and to deepen, we need to use our power to inquire, wonder, explore and see what is true for ourselves. Open to the messiness, discordance, ambivalence, and vital life force of questioning. With faith we welcome the ever-changing flow of life with all of its movement and possibilities. Faith is the capacity of our hearts to be in the present and find the underlying thread connecting the moment's experience to our threads of life. It opens us to the bigger sense of what we are and what we are capable of being.

Today's Quilt Making

Quilts have returned to mainstream American life. We see them at every turn—on television, in movies, as wall hangings, book covers, and clothing designs, and of course, on beds. Quilts are visually appealing. Their colors, textures, warmth, and versatility represent the perfect complement to contemplative living.

With the Bicentennial in 1976, the American handicraft movement was reborn. The craft fairs that are so prevalent today got their start in the late seventies. This movement signals the modern-day developments of quilt making. Today, there is a whole world of quilting inspiration available for us to draw on, including exhibitions, shops, books, national organizations, local groups, and websites. All kinds of innovations, such as specialized tools, instruction techniques, and contemporary patterns, are available. There are tremendous educational opportunities in classes, workshops, travel, and competitions. We can see exhibitions of antique quilts or contemporary quilts that use quilting as a fine art medium.

There are as many ways to approach quilt making as there are people. For some readers, it will be the perfect leisure-time activity for artistic expression, while others may prefer the practical nature of the product. Some may decide this is worthy of a lifetime of work, while others will stop with a quilt for one bed. Some will choose complicated designs and materials and acquire sophisticated skills, while others will work to the bare requirements just to get a usable product. Some will purchase special fabrics and materials, and others will use only what is on hand. Some may never make a quilt from this book, while others will make these projects ten times over. My goal is to expose you to the world of possibilities, so that you can make a conscious choice of what you truly need. Anything is possible.

ONE-PATCH UTILITY QUILT

A 60-degree diamond tied quilt is a very nontraditional choice for a first project. Actually, because it's tied it's not a quilt at all but a comforter. It won its place here in this initial chapter because of its quick and impressive results.

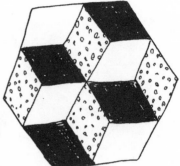

Baby's block hexagon.

The 60-degree diamond is a dynamic design within which any and all colors work together as long as we have the three values of light, medium, and dark. Depending on how the light, medium, and dark values are arranged, we can either see a six-pointed star, a three-dimensional cube, or some of both. The quilt example shown here has both arrangements, so the viewer sees a random pattern of stars and cubes. If you want cubes, piece the patchwork in blocks, always keeping the light at the top of the block, the medium on the left side of the block, and the dark on the right side. For the best representation of a star, use mediums for the star itself with either darks or lights for the surrounding background diamonds.

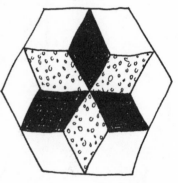

Star hexagon.

A 60-degree diamond necessitates piecing angles. The piecing can be done by hand or machine. The secret to nice sharp angles is to run the sewing machine needle right to the turning point. Leave the needle in the fabric and lift the presser foot. When working by hand, take a little backstitch at that point. In either case, arrange the second side of the angle so that the raw edges are even and lie flat so the fabric doesn't pucker at the turning point. (See illustrations on p. 32.)

Whether you decide on cubes or stars, piece the individual patches into hexagons, piece the hexagons into rows, and piece the rows together. A hexagon for a single cube is three patches. A hexagon for a star is twelve, six for the star and six around the outside of the star. The rows will be offset so that one hexagon falls to the right or the left of the one in the row above it. That necessitates half hexagons at both ends of every other row.

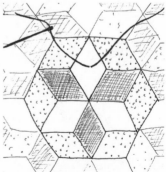

Tying a quilt.

Tying is a basic utilitarian finish, and the finished product is called a comforter because it is not quilted. Tying is a technique to hold all three layers of the quilt (the top, the batting, and the backing) together. Yarn is taken through the layers of the quilt from the top through the backing of the quilt and brought back up to the top, then tied in a secure knot before being trimmed. The ties are repeated at regular intervals throughout the quilt. Spaces between the ties should be 6 inches or less. It's easy, quick, and gives a wonderful additional texture to the finished product.

The yardages given below are for a 58-inch-wide by 70-inch-long quilt. Follow these recommendations if you want to buy cotton yard goods. However, you may like to try the material I used instead. I went to my local thrift store and purchased ten articles of various colored corduroy clothing.

Supplies

2 yards each light-, medium-, and dark-valued fabric

4 yards 45-inch-wide corduroy or flannel for backing

Twin size batting

Sewing thread or hand-quilting thread

Yarn to match backing

Yarn darning needles called sharps with a big enough hole for the yarn

Turning a corner.

Directions

1. Cut 3-inch 60-degree diamonds by first cutting 3-inch strips and then establishing the 60-degree angle at the end of the fabric and cutting the diamonds from that angle. You should find a 60-degree angle on your cutting board. If you don't have the angle on your board, can use a 30-60-90 plastic triangle available at any office or art supply store.

2. Piece the diamonds into either cube or star hexagons. Piece the hexagons into rows and then piece

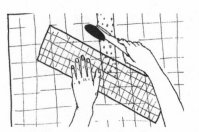

Cutting a diamond.

the rows together. For the quilt pictured, there were 15 rows alternating between 10 complete cube hexagons in a row and 9 complete cube hexagons with two halves at either end.

3. Press the completed patchwork from the front.

4. Piece the backing as necessary to be at least 7 inches larger all the way around than the patchwork.

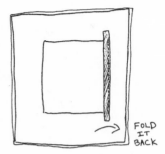

FOLD IT BACK

5. Lay pieced backing wrong side up. Cover with batting. Center patchwork right side up on top of batting.

6. Pin through all three layers wherever the ties will be made, using safety pins or long quilter's straight pins.

7. Make ties using yarn and a yarn needle. Double knot each tie. It may be necessary to use pliers to get the needle through all the layers.

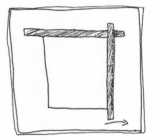

8. Add the first inside border. Cut 2-inch strips and piece as necessary. Attach the border, first the long sides and then the short sides, right sides facing to the patchwork top using the quilt-as-you-go method stitching through all the layers at once: the border, the patchwork, the batting, and the backing. Press border flat to the right side.

9. Add the second border from the 4½-inch strips using same quilt-as-you-go method. Press the border flat to the right side.

Adding a border.

10. Cut the batting to match the top. Cut the backing 2 inches larger than the top and the batting all the way around.

11. Bind by folding in the backing twice, first to meet the raw edges and a second time to cover raw edges of top and batting. Stitch along folded edge through all layers.

Variations

I tried to count the number of times I've made a variation of the 60-degree diamond and got to over two dozen when I decided that's enough to make my point. One of the greatest things about quilting compared to other forms of needlework is its versatility. Each of the projects included here can be done infinite times with infinite variations. It becomes your responsibility to decide what works for you. If for any reason you find this project or any of the others too ambitious, try the technique on a smaller piece that can be used as a wall hanging, throw, or even a placemat. Smaller projects build confidence. As your confidence increases, choose any of the following ideas to broaden your experience:

- Change the size of the 60-degree diamond to either larger or smaller by changing the width of the strips you cut.

- Make the comforter again in a different size or different materials.

- Instead of tying it, machine or hand quilt your top. This is best done with cotton yard goods that are made to be quilted.

- Use the patchwork top as yardage to construct a garment with a clothing pattern.

THE CONTRAST OF FEMININE AND MASCULINE

Log Cabin Quilt

Binah: *understanding; the ability to extract and connect information from the logical system of the laws of nature.*

I grew up in the American model family of four in the 1950s. We were composed of one breadwinning dad, one housewife mother, one older brother, and one younger sister. We had one car, one bathroom, and a rotary telephone with one extension in the kitchen and the other in my parents' bedroom. We had sidewalks, stop signs, and a neighborhood shopping area with an Italian grocery, a Jewish grocery, a drugstore with a soda fountain, a bakery, and a kosher butcher. I shortened the five-block walk to my grade school by cutting through my aunt's yard. My main form of entertainment, other than watching a black-and-white TV, was hanging out by myself at our local playground right across the street from our house. My mother's mother, Nana, lived with us. She and I shared a bedroom.

My dad, his two brothers, and his father worked long hours operating a retail business. My mom was a traditional homemaker. She did not work outside the home. She was responsible for all our basic physical needs, such as buying our clothes. She handled all the household affairs, including paying the bills. My mother arranged my parents' social events with similar couple friends who had all grown up together and had attended the same public schools as I did.

My brother was naturally athletic. He participated in all kinds of different sports and received state recognition for his tennis prowess. I had ballet and piano lessons and was not particularly good at either. When I was eight, my mom's cousin became a knitting teacher at a local knit shop. I went there after school and learned basic knitting. I caught on quickly and became particularly enamored with a mitten pattern, making probably a half dozen with leftover red acrylic yarn. My mom did all kinds of needlework: knitting, needlepoint, rug hooking, cross-stitch quilt tops (which she had quilted by a local church group), and table cloths. She was always doing something to occupy herself, even if it was the card game solitaire. Every Sunday, we went with our cousins to my father's parents' apartment for the usual meal of chicken soup, corned beef, chopped liver, chocolate gem cupcakes, Juicy Fruit gum, and M&M's.

All my female role models were conventional women in traditional roles with one exception—my dad's cousin, Sis. She had a family, but she also had a business with two other male cousins, and so in addition to being a mother/house-wife, she was also a businesswoman. She seemed kind of manly to me because she wore pants and always had a ciga-rette hanging out the side of her mouth. We only saw her at infrequent cousin meetings, but I was always interested in her and wondered about how and why she was different.

Like most young girls my age, I used to look forward to the Miss America pageant every fall. I aspired to be a contestant, and constantly wondered what talent I would demonstrate. In seventh grade when I started sewing, I would fantasize about an onstage fashion show. It seemed the only possible true talent I possessed, but I feared it was so different from the conventional baton twirling that it would never fly. One time when I was in high school, some women staged a protest outside the pageant on the boardwalk of Atlantic City. They burned their bras. It sounded like a wild and crazy idea to me. What were they thinking? What did bras have to do with anything?

There you have it: my traditional American family with very time-honored gender roles. The thought never occurred to any of us, including me, that I could or should be or do anything differently. My big dream opportunity for my future came in high school with my sweetheart, who was an all-star baseball pitcher. I spent my time fantasizing that he would become a professional baseball player, and I would become his famous wife by selling laundry detergent on television commercials.

Yet for all the external perfect traditional family values, there were underlying signs of dissatisfaction that looking back show why the idyllic fifties gave way to the turbulent sixties and the redefining of traditional gender roles. Our roles provided an artificial balance. Each of us had no choice in who we would become, and by staying within the limits of these specific gender roles, we each suffered. For myself, I had no concept that I had any talent or skills to offer the world other than to stand beside my high school sweetheart and look cute. What developed was a true underachiever with a weak self-image and much unrealized potential. The life-altering sixties changed everything.

Binah's Plurality of Forces

Binah, understanding, is the uppermost feminine element, standing near the top of the Tree of Life as the primordial mother. *Binah* is divine intelligence in which hidden patterns achieve concreteness and form. She is the analytic and distinguishing aspects of divine thought, including processed wisdom or deductive reasoning.

Together, *chochmah* and *binah* manifest the core model of intellectual balance. *Chochmah*, wisdom, starts as formlessness, develops into a point, and then becomes differentiated through the power of *binah*. An idea generated by *chochmah* is raw and not particularly feasible or useful. I am drawn to fiber and quilts. If we analyze that idea's ramifications and applications, asking about its parameters and truths, we are using the divine attribute of *binah*. If I think, "A quilting group with my friends could be a fun way of learning to quilt," *chochmah* is the conception; *binah* is the analysis. *Chochmah* is the masculine mode of cognition; *binah* is feminine intuition. With *chochmah* and *binah*, we have the concepts of discernment and comprehension coming together as one.

Our brains use the interplay of *chochmah* and *binah*. *Chochmah* is the original flash of insight, the concept. It is the thrill of a new quilting idea, flashing through our minds, showing us how engaging in our favorite activity can foster integration. When struck by this new insight or concept, we are in *chochmah*. Conception is thrilling, but it's a far cry from understanding, let alone developing and executing an idea. *Binah* takes that flash of insight, elaborates it, and probes its particulars. *Binah* is every thought process that unfolds in our minds. It is the meticulous systemizing and quantifying of the conceived solution. *Binah* is rational intelligence manifested in the way philosophers and writers use language to explore the nature of the universe. We grasp a solution and experience the thrill of receiving it. We know we've come across something grand and wonderful, but do not yet realize the details of the solution. *Binah* is the elaboration, understanding the aspects and particulars of the plan, idea, or solution. *Chochmah* encompasses the entire idea enclosed in a nutshell. *Chochmah* remains elusive without the grounding of *binah* figuring out how the details will come to play. On the other hand, *binah* cannot formulate without the illumination and inspiration of *chochmah*. *Binah* is differentiation and the beginning of separation. The potential of *binah* allows us to develop self-control, impersonal understanding, and objective love. It also has a dark side, allowing willfulness and evil to enter the universe.

While both men and women use *chochmah* and *binah* in each and every part of their thinking process, the masculine mode excels at *chochmah* while the feminine mode excels at *binah*. That's why we refer to male intelligence and female intuition.

Feminine Faces of the Divine

The Divine is infinite, formless, and genderless. As part of its totality, it must include both male and female. As we desperately try to comprehend the Divine, we ascribe human qualities to help us understand. The most obvious is to give the Divine a gender.

There are hundreds of thousands of female divine images. Quan Yin is one of the most universally beloved of deities in the Buddhist tradition. Also known as Kuan Yin, Quan'Am in Vietnam, Kannon in Japan, and Kanin in Bali, she is the embodiment of compassionate lovingkindness. As the bodhisattva of compassion, she hears the cries of all beings. Quan Yin enjoys a strong resonance with Mary, the Mother of Jesus, and the Tibetan goddess Tara. In many images, Quan Yin is depicted carrying the pearls of illumination and pouring a stream of healing water from a small vase. This water blesses all living things with physical and spiritual peace. She holds a sheaf of ripe rice or a bowl of rice seed as a metaphor for fertility and sustenance. The dragon, an ancient symbol for high spirituality, wisdom, strength, and divine powers of transformation, is a common motif found in combination with this goddess of mercy. Sometimes Quan Yin is represented as a many-armed figure, with each hand either containing a different cosmic symbol or expressing a specific ritual position, a *mudra*. One such *mudra* with cupped hands symbolizes the womb as the door for entry to this world through the universal female principle. This characterizes the goddess as the source and sustenance of all things.

Quan Yin originally lived on earth as Miao Shan, a young woman of unearthly virtue. Although her father wished her to marry, Miao Shan decided to visit a monastery. Contrary to her expectations, it was a hotbed of vice. Her father, hearing of her presence in the monastery and fearing his daughter's fate, burned it to the ground. A rainbow carried her to heaven, where her innocent death earned her transmutation into the divine world. Quan Yin is an enlightened being, an example of a bodhisattva who vows to remain in the earthly realms and not enter the heavenly worlds until all other living things have completed their own enlightenment. She is so concerned for humanity that upon receiving enlightenment, she chose to retain human form rather than transcend as pure energy. With this commitment, she remains but is liberated from the pain-filled cycle of birth, death, and rebirth.

Another Divine Mother is Our Lady of Guadalupe, the patron saint of Mexico City. It is said that she can cure almost any sickness. A Mexican named Juan Diego saw a striking woman who revealed to him that she was Mary, Mother of Jesus. As a sign, she put a handsome image of herself on a very thin cloth. This cloth can still be seen today in the Basilica of Our Lady of Guadalupe in Mexico City.

In Hindu tradition, Kali is a goddess who emanated from the brow of the goddess Durga, slayer of demons, during one of the battles between the divine and antidivine forces. Durga's name means "beyond reach" or "invincible." She personifies the woman warrior's courage and autonomy as well as being a Mother Goddess. Kali emerges as the forceful form of Durga, with her sword and her necklace of skulls. She is a fierce protector.

Universal awareness of the female divinity in all beings elicits tenderness, respect, love, and caring. We associate these Divine Mothers with the widespread experience of the holiness in all the earth. Gaia is known as Mother Earth. She was an early earth goddess born from chaos, the great void of emptiness within the universe.

Artemis of Ephesus, layered in rows of nurturing breasts and surrounded by animals, awakens the nurturing force of nature. Other prehistoric wide-hipped, full-bodied fertility goddess figures restore faith in the sacred beauty of the female body and its life-giving powers embodying maternal protection.

The many stories and anecdotes featuring female deities serve to convey the idea of enlightened beings who embody the attributes of an all-pervasive, all-consuming, unwavering loving compassion accessible to everyone. They counsel us by their actions to cultivate within ourselves particular qualities of mercy. Contemplating these goddesses involves little dogma or ritual. The simplicity of these loving beings and their standards leads us toward a more compassionate and loving self, which in turn naturally develops a deep sense of service to all our member beings.

Unfortunately, being steeped in a traditional Jewish childhood did not expose me to these female images. My upbringing was quite definitive that the Divine is a male deity. Even as an adult, when I heard the word *God*, I pictured that illustrious, bearded old king sitting on a throne in the clouds. I had heaps of trouble relating to this vengeful male authority figure, and then my adult religious explorations brought me to *Shechinah*.

Shechinah is derived from the Hebrew word *shaken*, meaning "to dwell." The term refers to the in-dwelling feminine face of the Divine. It is a limited form of the divine light that is accessible to us. *Shechinah* can be compared to the moonlight that—unlike the sun—we can look at directly. Traditionally, she is shown sometimes as a bride and at other times as a mother. She is the most literal comprehensible part of our relationship with the Divine.

On a practical level, she is a window into our internal spirit facilitating the discovery of a more personal relationship with a maternal aspect of the Creator. *Shechinah* is the beacon of spirituality that brings us closer to the loving, tender, and compassionate role of spirit within each of us.

The Hebrew language has both masculine and feminine forms. Often the patriarchal language in traditional liturgical Hebrew prayers refers to the Divine in the masculine singular, and that does not sit comfortably with me. As a maternal figure, *Shechinah* is the portal to move beyond the narrow view of a male deity's malevolence. *Shechinah*'s manifestation clarifies my broader question of gender differentiation and equality, allowing the concept of the Divine as a loving entity incorporating both male and female elements. Walking hand in hand with *Shechinah* expands access to the divinely inspired attributes of human compassion and tolerance in our society. *Shechinah* provides me access to the religion of my birth, affirming what I know as truth: The Divine is totally beyond gender, incorporating female as well as male into oneness.

In *Shechinah*'s positive image as a Divine Mother, she represents the sexual union with the Divine Father. Acceptance of the body as sacred is central to all religious practices. Many of the teachings of divine aspects and attributes are in the form of erotic metaphors because they are easily recognized and understood. Traditional writings illustrate that holy men have had difficulty coming to terms with their sexual needs and desires. They felt ambivalent about their sexuality and women's roles. They established and enforced many regulations and forms of denial concerning sexuality. It is our responsibility to challenge and go beyond these limited metaphors and interpretations and find our personal *Kama Sutra* (an ancient Sanskrit treatise on the art of love and sexual technique) that will facilitate locating the oneness, a wholeness of sexuality for our individual needs in this private part of our lives.

We are fortunate to be able to turn to feminist spirituality and goddess-inspired practices to help us cherish our physical incarnation in all its richness rather than the monastic ideal of renunciation in which instinct and desire are viewed as a hindrance to divine union. Sexual relations, childbirth, and breast-feeding, along with all the desires and needs of the body, are considered holy rather than sinful. In this sense, imagining the Creator as a woman awakens the part of us that is endlessly imaginative and regenerative. From this point of view, the children we raise, the dishes we cook, and the quilts we make become living prayers of the Divine Feminine. Each is a colorful celebration of the miraculous gift of life's creations.

From a theological perspective, a feminine-based contemplation deepens our capacity for a faith based on inner knowing, rather than external doctrine. It means acceptance of things as they are, rather than how we want them to be. It is about connecting to the cyclic wisdom in the rhythms of nature, in which things change and evolve in their own good time. By restoring the divine feminine principle to our spiritual lives, we help to heal an old wound, redressing history's omission and making ourselves whole. This step-by-step shift from the masculine to the feminine can even affect how we contemplate the formless aspect of the Divine. The mystical experience of oneness becomes less like the void of emptiness and more like swimming in a sea that is vibrant with potential life. In my own deepest moments of mystical participation with the divine feminine, I am bathed in waves of joy with happy sounds of laughter as the background hum of all creation.

Every divine aspect including *Shechinah* has a dark side. She is not only all light and love but can be out of balance and instead exhibit stern judgment. *Shechinah* can become malevolent and turn from a source of life and love to a source of death and hate. We must remember that wholeness contains everything, including darkness and evil. The major problem with using any gender association like *Shechinah* is that we risk locking ourselves into another one-dimensional understanding of the Divine except that now we are looking from the other side. A concept of the *Shechinah* that transcends gender is to see her as the literal divine presence within each of us. We become the vehicle of *Shechinah* holding the divine presence in this world. The messianic era involves the unification of consciousness across all boundaries, genders, ethnic identities, and religions. That collective awareness based on the unity of all beings with the Divine through a personal relationship fosters respect for the beauty of difference, allowing humanity to enjoy mutual tolerance and compassion.

Discovering the female aspect of the Divine is our hidden treasure. It broadens and enriches our spiritual understanding of the power of balance, intimacy, and creation. All names for the Creator are inadequate, but having both a masculine and a feminine depiction gets us closer to balance and complete wholeness. The symbolic language of the female is a deep underground river that unites the subconscious of humanity. Using a divine name that is inclusive of the male and female principles takes us another stitch along our quilting path.

Our challenge in creating a spiritual life is to maintain the healthier aspects of gender balance. The healthy masculine is benevolent, generous, playful, and flirtatious. That masculinity supports purpose with the capacity for focus and action. Add in the feminine power that engages personal empowerment, and we have a two-part effort combining to strengthen us individuals, our roles and voices in the universe.

How will we accomplish this in quilt making? By emphasizing process rather than product. We focus on the positive traits with a heightened recognition of our value in relationships, the contributions we can make. We express and celebrate beauty, collective intelligence, transparency, intuition, and humility. Fears indicate where deep feelings lie. We translate our fears into fierceness, and we transform at the powerful intersection and combination of masculine and feminine.

Log Cabin Quilts

Quilt names were never very complicated. Most often quilters adopted a name that referred to something in their daily lives. It is easy to bring to mind the visual reference of quilt patterns such as Pinwheel, Lone Star, Bow Tie, Drunkard's Path, and Tree of Life.

The popular and easily recognizable log cabin pattern is a quintessential American quilt design. The Log Cabin Quilt represents the home. Its construction came from the colonial quilt maker's direct experience of building a log cabin house, which works from a center block.

The heyday of the Log Cabin Quilt occurred in the latter half of the nineteenth century, corresponding to the widespread trek westward after the Civil War. In this era of quilting, as in early colonial times, there was a genuine scarcity of usable cloth.

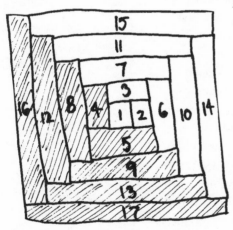

Log Cabin block with 4 logs per side.

Quilts were often made from worn-out clothing and other cloth. As part of the tradition, red-colored center squares represent the hearth fire and yellow-colored centers represent the lantern in the window.

Once the center block is established on a precut foundation block, light color values are placed on two sides of the block to represent the sunny side of the house and dark values on the opposite two sides for the shady side of the house. Strips are added in sequence around the sides of the square, varying the values between light and dark. The blocks can be set together in many ways and varying patterns of light and dark. Some block arrangements have their own names such as barn raising, sunshine and shadow, straight furrow, and pinwheel.

Pinwheel pattern.

Simple construction gives a wide freedom in selecting materials. The pattern works with scraps as well as planned yardage. It appeals to beginning and advanced quilters alike because the design and its variations are incredibly versatile, allowing for a result that can be contemporary, traditional, or primitive. I can safely say this is the pattern I most often refer to and rely on for consistently successful results. The Log Cabin never disappoints me.

Early blocks were almost always pieced on fabric foundations, and that is the technique we will employ. The older Log Cabin Quilts were usually not color coordinated. The secret is the strong division of lights and darks. A consistent center also helps carry our eyes along the quilt. Since the blocks were made of narrow strips of fabric, sewing them together on a foundation provided the necessary precision as well as stability. This technique, called pressed piecing, was developed before the invention of batting. The layering and folding of the cloth create a thickness and warmth without a third layer added in the middle.

Again, as in the last project, this Log Cabin Quilt will be tied to its backing: With all of the thickness of the folds and the foundation block, it would be next to impossible to quilt. Being tied allows the quilter to use fabrics of different weights and recycled cloth.

TWIN-SIZE FOLDED LOG CABIN QUILT

The Log Cabin sample shown here is a twin-bed size made of 140 blocks, 10 blocks across the width of the bed and 14 blocks made along the length. The finished measurements will be 57 inches by 77 inches, covering a twin mattress that is 39 inches by 75 inches.

This quilt can be pieced by hand or machine. I love the pressed piecing technique for beginners, as none of the stitches show on the finished quilt. It's a nice opportunity to gain experience and confidence without the worry of poor stitching. Old sheets work great for both the foundation blocks and the backing, as long as they don't have too high a thread count, which is difficult to get a needle through.

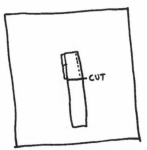

Supplies

3 yards foundation fabric (You can buy muslin yard goods for this or use any larger pieces of leftover fabric available. I cut up and used obsolete men's dress shirts.)

⅓ yard solid for the centers

6 yards both lights and darks

5 yards backing fabric

Tying yarn, color coordinated to the backing

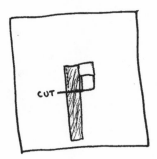

Directions

1. Cutting: Select and divide fabrics into either lights or darks. Cut into 1½-inch strips across the width of the cloth. Cut 1½-inch-square centers. Cut 6-inch-square foundation blocks.

2. Piecing block: Center the center square over the foundation block, right sides up. Place the first light log strip right side facing the foundation block, along one edge of the center square, covering the square. Stitch. Fold back so the right side of the log is showing. Cut away the excess of the log strip. Make one quarter turn, and lay the same light over

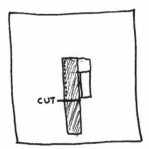

Building a Log Cabin block in steps.

both the center square and the first light—right sides together. Attach this second log stitching through all layers. Turn to right side. Take first dark strip, make a quarter turn of the block, and place this one right side down to form the third log. Stitch and turn. Complete one round with the same dark, right sides together, stitching through all layers and turning to right side. This completes one round of logs. Continue in this manner for four rounds of logs, working clockwise around block, laying wrong sides together, stitching, cutting, and finger pressing until all logs have been added.

3. Piece quilt top: Arrange the blocks. Chain piece blocks into rows, and then stitch rows together to complete top. Press from the front.

4. Finishing: Piece the backing as necessary. It needs to be at least 3 inches larger than the top all the way around the outside edges. Pin layers together where there will be tying, and complete the tying going up and back through all the quilt layers, using a double knot. Trim the backing to 1½ inches larger than the top on all four sides. Enclose the raw edge of the backing by folding it over twice to the front of the quilt, and then machine stitch through all layers.

5. Sign and date your quilt. You can use embroidery floss or a permanent ink marker.

Variations

- Make this quilt in a different size. Start with the mattress dimensions. A baby quilt is 26 inches by 52 inches, a double is 54 inches by 75 inches, a queen is 60 inches by 80 inches, and a king is 78 inches by

80 inches. Measure your mattress and add additional inches for the sides of the bed and to cover the pillow. Each block's finished measurement is 5½ inches square. To figure the yardage for the 1½-inch-wide logs, allow one 45-inch strip of light and one 45-inch strip of dark per block. This is overly generous, but it makes the calculations easy and gives lots of choice as you get closer to the end of the block construction and some leftovers for complementary pillows or a throw.

Pineapple Log Cabin design.

- Use a different arrangement such as straight furrows or pinwheel for your blocks.

- Try the pattern again using a color combination such as blue and white instead of lights and darks.

- Use the leftovers for pillows or a throw, adding more lights and darks as needed.

- Use pieces of your old clothing. Strip them just as you would yard goods.

- Try the Pineapple Log Cabin design, a more complicated version of the Log Cabin. In this pattern, strips are laid on the diagonal in addition to those on the horizontal and vertical planes.

BINDING TOGETHER SKILLS

String-Pieced Pillows

Da'at: *knowledge; the tool of the intellect that gets us into action mode.*

One way of acquiring knowledge, *da'at*, is through teachers. When we open our eyes, we find teachers anywhere and everywhere, even with our pets. On October 25, 2005, I wrote an e-mail to my children:

Iz, E, Sar,

I slept in late this morning, odd dreams. Zoe waited patiently at the bottom of the steps and we ventured out into the rainy cold. When it was my turn for patience, it was not returned. I was quick with her to do her business and mad at myself that I hadn't been more warmly dressed.

When we returned, as Zoe ate and I made my coffee, the phone rang. It was the young woman who watched Zoe last week. "Is Zoe still up for adoption?"

I will backtrack here to tell you that Zoe spent the week before last with this woman, her man, and Milo, a five-year-old fawn pug. They live in a beautiful house in Swissvale. Zoe had spent a happy week there, all of them sleeping in the same bed, romping in the enclosed yard, eating, playing with Milo and most of all being greatly loved and treasured by the woman herself.

The final day of the visit, Monday, the woman begged her man to let her keep Zoe. She even asked Zoe for confirmation and Zoe proceeded to do her howling trick. But it didn't work. To him, two dogs were more trouble than one and he didn't want to take Zoe on. So the woman took Zoe to the gallery where she works and called me to come and pick her up. When I arrived in the early afternoon Zoe was snoozing in her arms. It was a sad parting. They had fallen in love. "I'll watch her any time for you," the woman said.

Back at the loft, I sewed the rest of the day and Zoe did her usual, which as you know, is mostly sleeping in her crate. At one point she came to see what I was doing and I said to her, "We're back to the same old story, Zoe." She went back to bed.

Meanwhile, back at Milo's house, man and woman were lamenting their loss. Man said, "I've changed my mind. I see how much Zoe means to you and I'm honored that you respected my wishes and sent her back. You can bring her here to live if you truly love her and still want her."

So, children, it is time. Each of us has gone on to new experiences, new living situations and new relationships. It's Zoe's turn. The woman is wonderful and Milo, being a like-minded pug is a great match for Zoe. We are welcome to visit and I may even watch Milo and Zoe here sometime.

It's funny to feel this emotion that is welling inside me. Zoe represents our family life, the living remnant of all of those years together in your childhood home. We had a damn good life there, didn't we? Let's wish Zoe well as she goes on her way.

Love, Mum

Two weeks later, I wrote an e-mail to Zoe-dog herself, in care of her new family:

Dearest Zoe,

How is your new retirement life going? I wonder about you every day. I want to thank you for being my teacher. I am grateful to have been in relationship with you these past eight years. You taught me about consistency, stability, one-mindedness, and the true essence of living in the moment. Observing, interacting and caring for you helped me realize the extraordinary nature of ordinary life.

Please accept my deepest gratitude and my ever-increasing appreciation, I wish you long life and great happiness with your new family,

Mum

So there you have it. I finally did what I've wanted to do since the day I got Zoe-dog—find someone other than myself to take care of her. From the day she arrived at our home, I resented Zoe's total dependence on me. Zoe was my fourth child, and I was quite purposeful in my decision to stop after having three.

Some people have suggested that for my one-dog experience, a pug was the wrong breed. The breed was a family decision, a pug being everyone's second choice. My first choice was a papillon, those tiny beautiful dogs that are so small you can carry them in your pocket. *Papillon* is the French word for "butterfly." They are called as such because the ears look like butterfly wings. This breed is described in the textbooks as steady yet lively, vivacious and charming, and at the same time calm, patient, gentle, dignified, and obedient. Doesn't it sound like a great dog for me? However, this was the family's dog, and in the interest of family I agreed to Zoe. In retrospect, there is no denying that everyone's second choice is no one's first. That became the crucial issue on this bottom-line decision to let her go on her way.

Zoe was a lot of dog in a small space. She was noisy, silly, persistent, rambunctious, perky, and easily overheated. The dog books describe pugs as clever and mischievous with a heart-winning personality. Zoe required attention. She was her own style of willful, but I had won the battle on that issue and had her pretty well trained. We only went outside twice a day. She would sit nearby afterward waiting for however long it took me to put food in her bowl and give her permission to begin eating. She never climbed on the furniture, was not allowed on the second floor of the house, slept in an open crate, and always sat patiently by the door whenever I left the house to see if she might have the good fortune to be included in the adventure.

What led me to parting from her was that Zoe made it clear her relationship with me was based solely on what she could get out of it for herself. She had absolutely no concern or care for me and my needs. Whenever she was in the room, on a walk, or driving in the car, the story became all about Zoe. Quite frankly, with my youngest adult child leaving the homestead to live in New York, there was no incentive for me to keep Zoe around.

My first week without Zoe, I hit a bump. I had lost my reason for getting out of bed in the morning. I suddenly understood how Zoe had framed my day, my week, and all my basic physical life actions. She had given me a system that worked for both of us, getting up at the crack of dawn and ending the workday at sundown. I missed her most because of her requirement to go outside for exercise and defecation. Zoe's regular eating, regular elimination, and a daily walk also worked for me. She gave me a daily structure that someone working alone at home craves.

I would be missing a large part of Zoe if I didn't mention that Zoe was my number one example of unconditional love. She constantly longed to be held, petted, scratched, and rubbed. It didn't matter what I did to or for her, she was right beside me wanting to please me, to love me consistently, always at my beck and call, and eternally open to any form of affection. While she took great care of herself, she also took great care of me.

Zoe taught me another important lesson, and that was the value of having fun. Zoe was absolutely always up for an adventure. It didn't matter the time of day or night, if there was bright sunshine or gloomy clouds, she was in for an enjoyable time. She was forever hopeful, hell bent on enjoying anything that crossed her path. Our walks ranged from a simple leash-bound saunter to take out the garbage to a free rein romping through the grass at our family cemetery. Zoe had fun while getting me outside into the fresh air.

The list can go on and on. It turns out Zoe was my teacher. In every place and at every time, she was consistently Zoe. It didn't matter what changed around her, she was 100 percent Zoe. One of the most famous koans in the Rinzai Buddhist tradition is, Does a dog have Buddha nature? The answer is *mu,* no. The truth is they don't need Buddha nature; they are all dog, and it is right for a dog to be only a dog.

Zoe was my best teacher about daily living, but when it comes to quilt making, I can't give you a specific example of someone who inspired me. In fact, when I was getting my graduate degree in leadership, as my project I looked very carefully at the quilt-making industry to identify teachers and their personal expressions of leadership.

When I stepped into Leadership 101, I felt out of my league. The class was predominantly higher-level business professionals. We went around the room to introduce ourselves and state our professions and purpose for coming to the program. When my turn came, I sheepishly declared that as I worked by myself in a studio, I must want to lead myself. To my amazement I was practicing an existing form of leadership called self-leadership.

Self-leadership has been more broadly defined as the process of influencing yourself to establish the self-direction and self-motivation needed to perform. Research in leadership across a variety of educational and industrial settings has shown that the practice of effective self-leadership can lead employees to many benefits, including improved job satisfaction, self-efficacy, and mental performance. Behavioral self-leadership techniques involve self-observation, self-goal-setting, self-reinforcement, and self-correction. Mental self-leadership techniques involve examination and alteration of self-dialogue, beliefs and assumptions, mental imagery, and habitual thought patterns. Self-leaders find the natural rewards inherent in the tasks they perform.

In effective self-leadership, there is a coordinated effort between the individual and the group as a whole. Looking at quilt making in a historical perspective, we see a true example of self-leadership. Everyone made quilts. There were all kinds of rules, guides, support systems, and social structures for women to engage in the quilt-making process, and each woman made the choices that worked for her. Women worked independently, in their family units, with friends, and in the larger community group. There was a balance between the individual and her place in the group. Self-leadership does not require entirely autonomous behavior without regard to others. Nor does it require that the identity and value of each individual be entirely put aside in favor of the work group or organization. Rather, an effective self-leadership perspective encourages individuals to find their own personal identity and mode of contribution as part of a group or organization.

When I examined the modern quilting industry, I was disappointed to find the self-leadership format missing. Today's quilt-making teachers were employing other types of leadership. For the most part, books, classes, video, and TV focus on very specific patterns without encouraging independence and creative thinking. I myself had never latched onto one teacher, as I was reluctant to follow in another's footsteps without regard to my personal creative expression. Analyzing the industry's leadership showed me why that was so. Being a teacher in the field, I encourage students to become more creative quilt makers who employ self-leadership as the best blueprint for achieving the most authentic and personal results. This allows each of us to gather the support, encouragement, and knowledge we truly want and need.

The *Da'at* of Acquiring Knowledge

Looking back to the ten *sefirot,* we understand that these *sefirot* or attributes are pieces in the process that is the unfolding of the Divine in this world. *Da'at* is the tool that gets us into action mode, the bridge from the Divine to engagement. Without *da'at,* no matter how profound the idea, no matter how well developed it is logically, it will not turn to action. *Da'at* bridges the awesome gap between concepts and reality. *Da'at* takes the germ of the idea from *chochmah,* combines it with the developed thought from *binah,* and allows us to put it all together into motion.

An example may help. You are reading this chapter and you realize that there is something to understand about how you gather information and what kinds of teachers work with your learning style. This idea is a flash of inspiration, previously a no-thought concept. This is the *chochmah* stage. Next you start to raise questions about this idea. What kind of learner am I? How do I lead myself? What can I use in this book to learn quilt making? This questioning, thinking, and debating is *binah.* You are taken with the idea and become convinced that you can learn to quilt using this book. You begin to take notes, discuss the ideas with others, purchase some fabric, and begin a project. Your original no-thought has transformed into an idea, and that idea goes beyond its abstract concept to become a concrete reality. This is *da'at.*

Da'at knowledge is achieved when we connect the dots between ourselves, others, and pieces of information. *Da'at* is not merely collecting facts; it is a coming together into intimate connection with them. *Da'at* is the intimate connection with knowledge.

To summarize the first three *sefirot* of the ten attributes:

- *Chochmah* is the spark of an idea, the initial form of raw data. The Kabbalah likens *chochmah* to a father who sows a seed that contains an undeveloped code full of potential. It is shown on the right-hand, masculine side of the tree.

- *Binah* processes and develops a concept, as a mother who nurtures and forms. It is shown on the left-hand, feminine side of the tree.

- *Da'at* is the concrete knowledge and consciousness and solid result: the birth of the quilt as a concrete bridge to the real world. Knowledge usually means knowledge about things outside oneself, but *da'at* is the knowledge of the one who knows the "I," the differentiated ego self.

It is a funny thing to know, truly know, oneself. It can even be a little frightening. We may not like what we see, but as we come into *da'at,* we are empowered. Without *da'at,* there is no accountability, no freedom, and no way to take our lives into our own hands. All these things become possible only when we look back at our own selves and ask the questions, "Why did I do that and not this?" "Is this really what I want to do?" "Is this really who I want to be?"

Gaining *da'at* is a gradual lifelong process. It is closely related to the development of language. By age three, most children have enough *da'at* to start learning the difference between right and wrong. We see this as our children enter into early childhood education. New discoveries of self continue throughout the stages of childhood.

In adolescence, *da'at* unravels from its cocoon, and a human being who finally begins to know and understand him- or herself emerges. Knowing is the source of everything. The kabbalists say that the world comes into being because the Divine knows it to be. Knowing is the fabric of which all things are made. Everything comes out of knowing.

Transmission of knowledge requires an active awareness and intention on the part of both teacher and student. The knowledge more often than not comes from the recognition of an absence, the shock of what is missing, and a lack of truth. Most teachers agree we need an emptying out, a letting go, to make space for the new understandings to appear. Ultimately, our lives are our teachers, and it is our choice how we integrate the learning.

Now we understand it is not the teacher we are talking about here but the recipient of the teaching. It never entered Zoe's mind that she was a teacher, yet for me to learn from Zoe, I had to open to the possibilities, to bring together my *chochmah, binah,* and *da'at* and figure out how I would live my daily life as my teacher, Zoe-dog, had taught me. It is only when our minds are open and receptive to learning and seeing that change can occur.

Repetition: The Key to Building Skills

Like many of us, I was not successful with my childhood piano lessons because I wouldn't take the time to practice. How many Thursday nights were spent in agony trying to prepare for the Friday lesson because that night was my first look at the music since the Friday before! In ninth grade, I came home from sewing class and asked my mom for a sewing machine. The first question out of her mouth was, "Would this be just like the piano and the guitar?" These were both big purchases and commitments on her part that I didn't honor with the required dedication. Thank goodness she gave me another chance.

Actively work on your motivation and energy, engaging your *da'at* as you embark on this project. Developing quilting skill requires commitment to the practice, to take the time and energy necessary to develop dexterity.

For quilt makers, repetition is the key. Each and every task is repeated endless times to combine seamlessly into the finished product. We need to discipline ourselves to keep doing the work, even when it becomes tiresome and tedious. There is no one standing by to keep us going. We set our own goals and time restraints. You may not like this kind of piecing. Do it anyway. It will build your skill, add to your comfort with the tools, and, as always, give you a pretty product that someone will treasure for years to come. From this moment forward, choose to stay with the present moment—embrace each strip as a new discovery, an opportunity to take a risk, build a skill, and foster a little piece of confidence in your ability to complete a task. The self-discipline and the self-leadership come with the commitment to carry out the project.

It will be helpful for you to protect yourself from interruptions and from conflicting commitments so that you can just be yourself, working on skill building without having to respond to others. Let your answering machine take care of the phone calls. Tell other family members that you need time alone, so that they understand they must wait for a given time period to request your services. Watch for all those deterrents that will keep you from getting at the project. Confusion, fatigue, depression, anxiety, and guilt will all rear their ugly heads if you allow them to. Don't let them. Have a wonderful time with yourself, your materials and tools, and your growing confidence as you follow your quilting path.

String Piecing

String piecing is recurring strips of patchwork that combine to create a whole. It is a good example of the underlying principle of repetition. String piecing is an easy way to create a fabric vocabulary. Cotton quilting fabric is cut across the width of the fabric, from one selvage to the other, into strips. Our quilting great-grandmas invented this method of piecing to use precious scraps and leftover fabrics. By stitching each little scrap of fabric to a foundation of paper or muslin, no pattern is required and every piece of fabric can be used with little waste. If you are lucky enough to find a vintage quilt top that was constructed using string piecing, you might even find a bit of the original newspaper still attached to the back of the quilt top.

Our pillow project will be foundation pieced on muslin so that we won't have to use up time picking and pulling away all those tiny pieces of paper on the back. Enjoy this introduction to string piecing, but I must warn you, you might find it addictive!

STRING-PIECED PILLOWS

The directions below are for two 14-inch pillows. The fronts are made using a muslin foundation string-piecing method. The backs are made from old front-button shirts. I came upon this idea when making memory pillows of others' materials. The first time, I used it out of necessity, having to do a commission easily and quickly within a limited time frame. Once I saw its beauty and ingenuity, I continued to use the technique for all my pillow projects, even when it meant sneaking into my daughter's closet or taking a quick trip to the thrift shop.

The key to the construction process is starting with a shirt. The best kind to use, particularly when you first try this method, is a man's dress shirt. It is big, with lots of well-placed simple buttons and a tight weave perfect for the wear and tear of a pillow. The buttons along the front closure of a blouse will also work as the closure for a pillow.

Supplies

6–8 ¼-yard pieces of quilter's cotton fabric. Do not use fat quarters, which are 18 inches by 22 inches. Instead cut the fabric along its width from selvage to selvage. Each piece will be 9 inches by 45 inches, a more usable piece of cloth for string piecing.

Two front-button man's cotton dress shirts—one for each pillow.

Machine sewing thread that matches the color of the shirt

Two 14-inch premade pillow forms

Directions

1. Begin by cutting the shirt apart. Cut off the sleeves. Cut up the side seams. Cut off the collar. Cut the back of the shirt into an 18½-inch square. If necessary, piece some of the sleeve fabric to the shirt-back to make it big enough. This will be the foundation lining and, at the same time, the pattern for the patchwork.

63

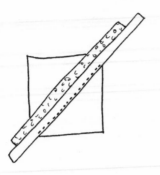

2. Button the shirt front and cut it into an 18½-inch square. Put this aside to be used as the back of the finished pillow. Again, if necessary, you can add some sleeve fabric to make it big enough. It's okay if the buttons don't go the whole 18½ inches, just so there are enough to allow you to unbutton them and insert the pillow form.

3. Cut the ¼-yard cotton fabric pieces into varying width strips. These strips can vary from 1- to 3-inch cuts across the 45-inch width of the fabric.

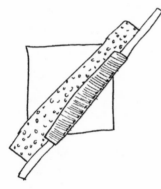

4. Lay out the square cut from the backing. Take one of the cut strips and lay it right side up across the diagonal of the square. Take a second strip and lay it right side facing the first strip. Stitch through all three layers.

5. Turn the second strip to show its right side. Press it flat. The sewn edge is now hidden. You now have two fabric pieces sewn to each other and the backing. Trim the strips on the edge to match the backing piece.

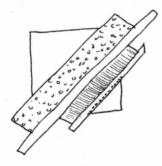

6. Continue the sewing/flipping/pressing, adding strips of fabrics, working toward the outer edges. You can work in both directions at the same time. Continue in this manner, following the diagonal line, until you have reached the two opposite corners. Use the full complement and variety of your fabrics. This will assure interest and contrast. Keep on in this fashion, adding different random-sized fabric pieces and working your way out from the center until the backing is completely covered.

String piecing on a pillow square.

7. When the top is completed and pressed, it is ready for the shirt-front backing. Place these together, right sides facing each other. Stitch ¼ inch around all four sides. Open the buttons and turn. Button and press the edges of the pillow from the right side.

8. Stitch 2 inches from the edge of the pillow through all the layers on all four sides, being careful not to hit any of the buttons. The measurements allow for a 2-inch flange edge around the perimeter of the pillow. Enclose the pillow form.

9. Repeat process for the second pillow.

Variations

- Change the size of the pillows by using different-sized pillow forms.

- Use the technique to re-cover a cushion in your home.

- Make several pillow tops as blocks that can be combined into a quilt.

- Try the technique with old pieces of your clothing. Strip them just as you would yard goods.

- Enclose batting between the foundation block and the string pieces to add more texture and warmth.

UNCONDITIONAL LOVE
Straight Furrows Patchwork Baby Blanket

Chesed: *love; unconditional giving; physically represented as the right hand.*

My middle child, Eli Michael, and his fiancée, Annie, planned a traditional wedding. They wanted a complete affair with all the trappings, including an engagement ring, formal bridal gown, bridal party, sit-down dinner, and a multitiered cake. At the same time, being children of the millennium, they produced their own website (Eli is the mastermind of my website), subscribed to an online bridal registry, and fashioned their personally distinctive computer-generated invitations. Because they met in an academic setting, they chose to exchange their vows in the open-air amphitheater of their alma mater's arboretum. Eli is my studious child with whom I love to engage in philosophical discussions. Being very familiar with my work, Eli is determined that I use his favorite techniques and materials to produce the ultimate wedding quilt as one expression of their commitment to each other.

The baby of our family, Sarah Lillian, is an aspiring artist who promotes her skills in Manhattan. She did the illustrations for this book. In the visual arts, she draws, paints, sculpts, knits, and quilts. She is in the process of hand quilting a queen-size log cabin quilt. Right out of the starting block, Sarah was interested in costume and performance. I can see her in my mind's eye at the age of six with her favorite toy, the family video camera. She would entertain herself for hours by performing to herself on the television monitor attached to our camera, which she was able hook up herself. Another favorite play activity was to make up stories using her Barbie dolls as the actresses. She reached some of her greater heights of youthful creativity when she transformed her Barbies into punk rockers, complete with dyed, spiked haircuts and nose rings.

There were many challenging moments with Sarah as she carried on with that uniquely creative mind of hers. When she was in junior high, she and I collaborated on an art exhibition as part of our annual local art festival. It was very frustrating for both of us. She was not at all interested in directions that I was compelled to supply. As a result, all we did was disagreeably butt heads. That experience and some serious soul searching taught me one important lesson of raising children—allow them to be who they are and not who we, the parents, want or need them to be.

Each of my children is very different from the other. I liken them to a 60-degree equilateral triangle. Their differences have helped me discover a wide range of parental roles, trying desperately to be the best mom possible no matter what the requirements. The one offspring responsible for keeping me most firmly planted on the ground at the base of my triangle is our firstborn.

Isadora Emily is learning disabled. She is what people term special. Isn't that a crazy way to say something isn't quite right? Aren't we all special? Doesn't each of us have our peculiarities and special needs? She has a cognitive audio deficiency that makes it impossible for her to learn by verbal instruction. She learns through action. Today, she does a great job employed as a cashier at a drugstore near her condominium. Her favorite leisure-time activities are bowling and needlecrafts. Her T-shirt collection is featured in the quilt for chapter 9.

Iz was a sweet baby, very passive and simply entertained. She didn't walk until she was nineteen months old. Starting as a newborn, there were a series of signs of her difficulties. At each juncture, she would be tested, with the results placing her at the very lowest end of the normal range. She consistently squeaked under the wire within the smallest of margins. In first grade she experienced such significant learning and behavior problems that another round of testing was suggested. With that arrived the diagnosis of "developmental delay." At this point in the story (well, to be honest, at all points in the story), I experienced frustration and anger. I didn't understand it then, but the diagnosis was a postponement of the inevitable. It was the professional cop-out of its day, not wanting to tell us the difficulties of her future at such an early life stage.

Then there were a series of special classes, tutors, and therapists, all with slightly less than desirable outcomes. When Iz reached eighth grade, I was panicked over the lack of appropriate high school options when I met the mother of an older child on a similar path. She gave me the video that changed all our lives.

The educator in the video managed to demonstrate to nondisabled students, teachers, and counselors how the learning disabled experience the world. The educator ran a school on Cape Cod. When we visited it, Iz wholeheartedly identified with the student population. Longing to fit into a group, she begged to attend. It was expensive, and it was very difficult to send a fourteen-year-old to boarding school, but it became our choiceless choice.

Those four years turned out to be some of her happiest. There she was captain of the soccer team and secretary of the junior class. She had lots of boyfriends and always went to the prom. It was a place of like-minded individuals who worked with each other in a supportive system to figure out what each could do best and how to take the next step of informing the larger population of their limits when they stepped beyond their insular world. The school did a superb job of providing tools that allowed for each individual's special needs to be clear and not hidden, and for each child to be accepted as he or she is.

The principal taught us the key to his success. He would only work with parents and children who were willing to accept fully who they are. Carrying out the school's philosophy in our home environment today, we treat each family member equally and fairly as a unique individual. What is appropriate for one might not be right for the other. The absolute bottom line is an original mind-and-action-altering definition of equality. Equal is not each getting the same, but getting what each needs.

Lovingkindness

The fourth divine attribute of the *sefirot* is *chesed,* or love. *Chesed* connotes kindness and altruism, an unconditional giving. True altruism is doing something without any expectations in return. *Chesed* teaches us to experience our feelings and promotes giving and sharing. *Chesed* is the idea of giving oneself totally.

Lovingkindness, unconditional giving, no boundaries, endless, ever-flowing all describe *chesed*. This kindness goes much deeper than just being nice and considerate. *Chesed* as a selfless loving action has no cause and no previous motive. It is like an anonymous gift of charity. Every action in the universe has a cause, except that which is first. A *chesed* act is not recycled. The ultimate *chesed* action, as an expression of expansiveness without cause, is the act of creation. Within the sphere of visible action, *chesed* is the initiator of interaction on that level of being seen. It is the primary spark that initiates subsequent action.

As with each divine attribute, there is a dark side. If we find ourselves totally dependent on another's approval for everything we do, or we are always looking for how others regard us and we can't seem to make independent decisions on our own, we have gone over the line into the dark side of *chesed*. Rage, terror, and instability are all symptoms that might indicate an imbalance in the *chesed* attribute.

Angels in Kabbalah

The Hebrew word for angel, *malakh,* or messenger, denotes the concept of transmission. The continual creation of the universe is a two-way dynamic relational process between the physical and the spiritual. Angels are the force of divine interaction that travels beyond the spiritual realm to our world. The Divine is always acting in the world guiding events based on our actions. It is a two-way process with a built-in feedback loop that allows for any necessary changes in programming. Angels are a conduit. Each angel transmits a unique quality and energy related to our spiritual growth. Angels send fragments of themselves to stand by and guide humans. It is possible to call upon any of the angels to assist in life's challenges. Being unconstrained by time or space, they are able to be with everyone who requests them simultaneously. This being their purpose, they are excited and eager to assist however they are able.

Friends and I have often joked about how I have a parking angel. Some have been concerned about wasting divine intervention on something as trivial as parking. Understanding that each angel is specific to a purpose changes the equation. It would be silly not to make use of the parking angel as that is its true and only purpose for existence.

There is a hierarchy of angels in scripture. Cherubim were the first angels to appear in the Hebrew Bible. They are a part of the inner circle of the Divine. The angel Metatron has a central role as the minister of wisdom, holding the keys to the mysteries of all divine matters. Mystics say that Metatron was created before anything earthly, representing microcosmic spiritual perfection free of impurities, a kind of archetype for angels.

Seated in the angelic inner circle are the archangels, who are created with tremendous bursts of life-force energy and gifted with absolute passion, perseverance, and unwavering devotion. Each archangel, like all the angels, has a specific mission related to our spiritual destiny and the fulfillment of our divine life purpose.

Michael, Gabriel, Raphael, and Uriel are the fabulous four archangels. Each has a distinct personality and vibration or feel. Archangel Michael, called One Who Is Like God, represents love. This angel of protection is the defender of light and goodness. A lion, the element fire, the direction south, the season autumn, and the color red represent Michael. This entity takes negatively minded people to the light so that their negativity is accepted. Michael clears negative energy from any space, including home, office, mind, and heart. We call upon Michael to assist us whenever we feel the presence of negative sources.

Archangel Gabriel, God Is My Strength, represents overcoming doubt and fear. Gabriel's element is water, the direction west, the season winter, and the color emerald. Gabriel is represented by the phoenix. This archangel messenger is the bearer of good news, whispering in our ear of coming events, changes, and opportunities for new experiences. Gabriel restores life and light into stale areas of our lives, such as relationships, businesses, and homes. Gabriel supports us as we resurrect blocked areas of our lives, filling us with the memory of our divine purpose and destiny and sending us creative ideas and opportunities to keep us moving and changing.

Archangel Raphael is the Shining One Who Heals. Raphael's element is air, the direction east, the season spring, and the color blue. Raphael is charged with the healing of our earth and all of her inhabitants. Raphael helps purify our minds and erase false beliefs that appear as thoughts. These are the triggers of many health problems. Symptoms give us clues of our physical blocks and imbalances. Both traditional and alternative healing facilities and practitioners receive guidance and help from Raphael. Raphael clears energy blocks so that health and vitality are our natural states of being. Raphael guides us with clarity and love in the healing process for others and ourselves.

Archangel Uriel, Fire of God, is the funniest and most easygoing of the set. Uriel represents clear thinking. Uriel's element is earth, the direction north, the season summer, and the color white. Uriel is represented by the bull. This archangel brings divine light into our lives, transforming painful memories and making peace with our past. Uriel turns our worst disappointments into our greatest blessings by working with us to release resentments that make us unable to forgive. Uriel enfolds us in waves of peace, anchoring us in love that is strong enough to withstand negativity.

There are hundreds of angels, but it is fun to include Jophiel in this discussion as our Angel of Creative Power. This light teaches our consciousness to discover the creative force within. Divine ideas begin to manifest as Jophiel's energy merges with our own creative divine essence and coordinates a team of powerful creativity angels to see each of our visions through to physical manifestation. Use Jophiel to fill your vision in each step of the quilt-making creative process.

Our final angel, Chamuel, the Angel of Adoration, anchors the essence of esteem to fill us with self-love and appreciation for all of our life gifts. To experience adoration for all of life we must experience all that life has to offer— even the more difficult lessons. With Chamuel's help, true feelings are no longer suppressed but instead are expressed. Chamuel cloaks us in the bliss of adoration and self-love.

We talked in chapter 1 of faith and trust. Faith is the beginning of understanding the Divine within. Faith also relates to the Divine without. Angels are an example. With everything we talked about so far, faith helps us in our process because it allows for a larger form of acceptance. I had a friend who always said, "If it's meant for you, it won't pass you by." Faith helps us identify the footprints of the universe sent to guide us.

What is grace? Grace also comes from the Divine. It always exists and is continually available to us. It's an actual connection to something greater than us. It's the feeling that emerges when we experience a sense of the miraculous, when we understand we are divinely guided and blessed, experiencing the Divine in us and around us. It is something we receive as the greatest act of lovingkindness.

Acceptance is experiencing a situation without any intention of changing it or any conception of the need for change.

Acceptance does not require that the situation be desired or approved by us. Acceptance is particularly useful when our situation is both disliked and unchangeable, or when change can only be achieved at great cost or risk. Acceptance implies not attempting a possible change, but it also suggests a more proactive stance, such as deciding to take no action for or against a situation. Acceptance is contrasted with resistance. Acceptance is sometimes used with notions of willingness. Even if an undesired, inescapable situation befalls us, we have the choice to willingly accept it or not.

We can accept various events and conditions in the world. Individuals and groups can accept their own thoughts, feelings, and personal histories. The Tibetan Buddhists, who were forced by the Chinese to leave their homeland and who currently reside in India, are an example of group acceptance. An individual example is encouraging a person with depression or anxiety to accept whatever personal circumstances have given rise to those feelings and to accept the feelings themselves. Buddhism's first noble truth, "Life is suffering," invites us to accept suffering as a natural part of life.

Lovingkindness Meditation to Open the Heart and Mind

Lovingkindness is a meditation practice taught by the Buddha to develop the mental habit of selfless and altruistic love. It brings about positive attitudinal changes as it systematically develops the quality of loving acceptance. It frees the troubled mind from its pain and confusion. Hatred cannot coexist with lovingkindness and dissipates if supplanted with loving thoughts. Lovingkindness has the immediate benefit of changing and sweetening old habituated negative patterns of the mind. Through this practice we befriend ourselves. The innocent mistake that keeps us in our own particular style of unkindness is that we do not see clearly what is. Our basic misunderstanding is the belief that by improving ourselves, by trying to be better than we are, we will avoid pain and be happy.

The original name of this practice is *mettabhavana,* which comes from the Pali language. *Metta* means love in a nonromantic sense—friendliness, kindness, or lovingkindness. We feel it in our hearts. *Bhavana* means development or cultivation. Lovingkindness meditation produces four qualities of love: *metta* or friendliness, *karuna,* or compassion, *mudita* or appreciative joy, and *upekka* or equanimity. The quality of friendliness is expressed as warmth that reaches out and embraces others. As our lovingkindness practice matures, it naturally overflows into compassion as we empathize with other people's difficulties. This positive expression of empathy is an appreciation of other people's good qualities or good fortune, or appreciative joy. It is not feelings of jealousy or pity. This series of meditations comes to maturity as equanimity. Ultimately, we remain kindly disposed and caring toward everybody with an equal spread of loving feelings and acceptance in all situations and relationships.

Lovingkindness meditation supports keeping an open mind. When I am troubled and people are getting on my nerves, I go to this practice. The first step to lovingkindness is loving myself. I am not being vain or selfish but attempting to generate my own sense of well-being and love of self. When in doing this I experience resistance, I recognize the presence of my very familiar feelings of unworthiness. The design of the practice helps me overcome my feelings of self-doubt or negativity. The practice goes on to develop lovingkindness toward others. There are three types of people to develop lovingkindness toward. The first is a respected or beloved family member, friend, or teacher. The next is a neutral person, somebody I know and have no special feelings toward, such as my neighbor or someone who performs a service for me. The third is a hostile person, someone I am currently having difficulty with.

Begin the practice by spending five minutes meditating at each stage. In the first stage, feel *metta* for yourself. Become aware of yourself, focusing on feelings of peace, calm, and tranquility. Let these feelings grow into feelings of strength and confidence, and then develop these into love within your heart. You can use an image such as golden light flooding your body. Or repeat a mantra or phrase over and over again, either out loud or silently, such as "May I be well and happy." Another method is making an affirmation, a positive statement about yourself in your own words. These are all ways of stimulating the feeling of *metta* for yourself.

For the next stage, think of a good friend. Bring them to mind as vividly as you can. Describe their good qualities. Feel your connection with your friend—how much you love him or her—and encourage these feelings of love to grow by repeating "May this friend be well and happy." You can also use the image of a light shining from your heart into your friend's heart, or form a mental picture of you and that person with a joyous feeling of love surrounding both of you. Reflect on the positive qualities of this person and the acts of kindness he or she has done. These visualizations and reflections are dependable devices for arousing positive feelings of lovingkindness. When the positive feelings arise, switch from the devices to the feeling. The feelings are the primary focus. Keep the mind fixed on the feeling. If it strays, bring it back to the device, or if the feelings weaken or are lost, then return to the device to bring back or strengthen the feeling. Use these techniques of a phrase, an image, or a feeling in the next two stages as well.

For the third stage, think of someone you do not particularly like or dislike, someone for whom your feelings are neutral. This may be someone you do not know well but have contact with. Reflect on their humanity and include them in your feelings of *metta*.

Next think of someone you actually dislike. Instead of getting caught up in feelings of hatred, think of this person positively and send your *metta* to him or her as well.

Finally, think of all four people together—yourself, the friend, the neutral person, and the adversary. Now extend your feelings further to everyone around you in your neighborhood, your town, your country, and so on throughout the world. Feel waves of lovingkindness spreading from your heart to everyone, to all beings everywhere. Then gradually relax out of meditation and bring the practice to an end. Systematically sending lovingkindness into the universe breaks down barriers. It will affect the divisions within your mind, which are the source of most conflicts.

How did it feel? Were you able to be with yourself without harshness or embarrassment? Did you discover a piece of your innate wisdom that exists along with your neurosis? Our brilliance, spiciness, and completeness is right beside our confusion, dissatisfaction, and harsh judgment. If we try to rid ourselves of our negative aspects, we also lose our wonderful idiosyncrasies and uniqueness. As your practice grows, your mantra will become: "I am grateful for who I am just as I am in this very moment." Cultivating gentleness and the ability to let go of small-mindedness opens our thoughts, emotions, minds, and hearts.

Lovingkindness is a heart meditation that can go beyond a sitting practice into everyday life. Take your experience into your home, your quilting, your neighborhood, and your relationships. Applying the practice to daily life is a matter of being friendly and open toward everybody you relate to without discrimination. One of my favorite activities is standing in the checkout line of the supermarket and sending lovingkindness to each person around me. With a little effort, the feeling becomes less discriminating—particular, preferential love, which is an attached love, becomes an all-embracing, unconditional love. It has no specific object and simply radiates feelings of universal love. Stick with the practice, and I promise you will be impressed with the results.

Life is messy. Figuring out what to accept and what to reject will be different for each of us. We can apply this to working with fabric with a moment of reflection, looking back, appreciating our process of growth as we learn about the many aspects of the quilting trade. How about a nice cup of tea as you peruse what you've created so far? Include not just the actual projects but also the different parts of the process including the space, the time, the tools, and gathering of the materials. You may be further along than you thought you'd be at this point. Then again you may be far behind. You are where you are and you are exactly where you are supposed to be. Be content in your acceptance of you as the quilt maker you are—exactly at this moment.

Baby's Blankie

Each of my children had a blankie, that piece of cloth that they clung to as a source of security. To this day, Isadora keeps hers under her pillow. With Eli, I saw his natural clinging nature, and I took the advice of a mother's magazine to cut the blanket in half, the notion being to continue cutting up the blanket until little remained of the original. Somehow I didn't get it right with Eli, because after I made the first cut, he joyously employed both blankies, and so the item had multiplied rather than divided.

With Sarah things got even more complicated when we were traveling overseas and realized the precious blanket had been left behind. That particular time she clung to the airport blanket. Another time she was in the hospital and adopted the pillow cover of the hot water bottle. Still another time she lost the blankie at a friend's house and reluctantly substituted one of her dad's old cotton tie-dyed T-shirts. This remains with her today—she has never totally accepted the loss of the original blanket. The first time I made one of these patchwork baby blankets, Sarah became convinced that one of the fabrics I wanted to incorporate was from her original blanket. I tried to persuade her otherwise, but it was useless. She squirreled the fabric away, and the only way I was able to retrieve it was by agreeing to make one of these blankets for her—complete with the bogus flannel. All these stories are by way of saying we all want this project to be the source of the baby's security and that special blanket that each will cling to long into childhood.

STRAIGHT FURROWS PATCHWORK BABY BLANKET

The directions are for a 36-inch square patchwork blanket. We will use the straight furrows block arrangement. In this arrangement the fabrics are offset by one on each row. This makes a diagonal pattern that reminds us of rows of planted fields.

Supplies

6 ⅓-yard pieces cotton flannel

1½ yards cotton flannel for backing

Sewing thread that matches backing

Directions

1. Cut the flannel into 2½-inch squares.

2. Arrange the squares into piles, one for each lengthwise row so that each specific fabric will be one square lower on each successive row. Repeat the fabrics in any order that suits you.

3. Chain piece the squares into rows. Begin with rows 1 and 2, and then go back and add row 3, and so on until you have completed 18 horizontal rows.

4. Sew the horizontal rows into sets of three. Flip the seams in alternate directions so that it is possible to match them without taking the time to pin them.

5. Using the quilt-as-you-go method, sew the remaining unstitched seams while at the same time sewing the patchwork to the backing. Start by laying the section with rows 1, 2, and 3 onto the backing wrong sides together allowing at least 2½ inches at each edge. Pin and sew the section with rows 4, 5, and 6 to section 1, 2, and 3 and the backing. Press to the right side. Continue stitching and pressing each of the remaining four sections.

6. Trim the excess backing to 1½ inches larger than the patchwork on all four sides.

Chain piecing squares into rows.

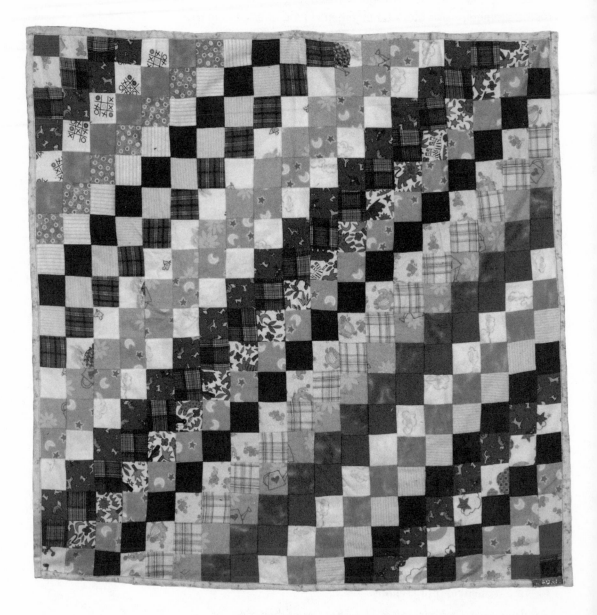

7. For the binding, do a double fold of the backing by turning in the raw edges twice and stitch through all of the layers at the folded edge of the binding.

Variations

- Save the extra squares to use with additional flannels when you want to make another baby blanket gift. Take advantage of your local fabric store's sales to stock up on flannel to use with the leftovers.

- Instead of using the quilt-as-you-go method, hand quilt the patchwork top with a batting and backing.

- Embroider the vital information about the baby onto the patchwork before doing the quilting.

- Try the technique with outgrown children's pajamas for the fabric. Cut squares from them just as you would from yard goods.

- Enclose an extra layer of flannel between the patchwork and the backing to add more texture and warmth.

BEARING OUR LOAD

Quilting Carry-all Bag

Gevorah: *restraint; an aspect of limitation; judgment; represented by the left hand.*

I am a walking advertisement for regular breast cancer screening. A routine mammogram revealed that I had a 0.77 centimeter malignant tumor. The whole affair occurred quicker than a wink. A sonogram and the biopsy were done immediately in the office at the time of the sighting. By the end of the following week, I had met with a surgeon and had scheduled an operation. By the end of the next month, I was cancer-free and undergoing radiation treatment and hormone therapy.

My treatment was and is nothing less than impeccable. We are fortunate in my town to have a women's facility that covers female health from birth to death. In the brightly lighted front entrance of the hospital, you are greeted by a grand player piano with beautiful inspiring music. There is always a genuinely smiling face saying good morning and answering any basic questions. The mix of teenagers, newborns and young parents, and the elderly accompanied by loving descendants is truly endearing. This atmosphere of caring people full of warm-hearted love allayed my cold-hearted fear about life-threatening illness.

When I made my first call to arrange to see the surgeon, the intake nurse asked all of those basic, very scary reality questions, but then she ended the conversation by assuring me of good care. She told me she was sorry we had to meet under these circumstances but that everything was going to be taken care of because I was in good hands.

A smile comes over my face as I think of all the bodhisattvas, beings that compassionately refrain from entering Nirvana in order to save others, associated with my health care in this supportive environment. One exceptional example of loving selfless care was my "breast man," as I affectionately referred to him. He and his two female technicians made the repetitive grueling drudgery of going to radiation every weekday for thirty-three treatments an odd form of pleasure. He and his colleagues engaged me personally and with a sincere humanity. We were simultaneously silly, serious, and practical, working on many levels with the underlying comprehension that this was all for my benefit. These interactions encouraged me to take on the treatment with a positive frame of mind, making all the difference between embracing life rather than fearing death.

When I first understood my predicament, there was an initial period of panic. I know survivors, but I have also been to the funerals of many women who died of this dreaded cancer. I had just entered a new relationship and wondered if I would be able to keep up my part of the bond.

Being the levelheaded type, I researched and found information that made me appropriately alarmed and at the same time able to seek and receive the necessary remedies. A tumor of less than one centimeter is very small. It is impossible to feel with a breast self-exam, one of the reasons a mammogram is a necessity.

I am terribly offended when I read about someone who "battled cancer." If there's a battle, there's a winner and a loser. I am not a good game player, and so I determined a different strategy. I made friends with my cancer, allowing it to teach me about my physical being and help me make lifestyle changes that would be to my long-term benefit.

By now I know myself well enough to understand what works and what doesn't. Keeping the wrong foods out of the house, making regular dates with walking partners, doing weight training first thing in the morning before the day gets in the way, outlawing evening snacking, and eating my bigger meal earlier in the day among other tools are things that work for me. Take my advice, on this one, do what I say and not what I do. I'm definitely a work in progress.

The *Gevorah* of Limiting Strength

Gevorah parallels the second day of creation, relating to barriers and restraints. On the Tree of Life it is opposite to *chesed*, giving without restriction. The idea of divine strength is not about brute force but rather the ability to withhold. If the Divine gave freely of itself, it would totally overwhelm us, and our world could not exist. If the Divine holds back completely, we would have nothing, and our world could not exist. For the world to be, *chesed* and *gevorah* balance each other through the constant harmonizing and interplay between the two. Pushing away means to extricate ourselves from feelings of independence, while drawing near illustrates the consciousness of interdependency. Law, strength, judgment, sternness, justice, hiddenness, boundary, restraint, fire, and ending are all words to describe the *gevorah* that helps us control our flow so that we know and do what is best for us.

The path between *gevorah* and *chesed* is symbolized by the Hebrew letter *aleph*. Its numeral value is one. *Aleph* is one of three mother letters corresponding to air. It relates to breathing yet it has no sound. It emanates from nothingness, the breath before creation. In nothing there is everything. We are touched with the infinite so we can create. Certain ways of breathing balance energies and help us overcome cravings, bad habits, and inertia. They open us to nothingness, which in turn opens us to oneness, love, and creativity. This helps us balance open lovingkindness with the closed restraint in all the worlds.

The negative side of *gevorah* is extreme self-judgment, feeling no right to be alive. The act of seeing through to our interior places is threatening. We need the love and understanding of *gevorah* to accept ourselves. We might think an easy solution to a negative *gevorah* is to add *chesed*, but this does not work. Pure *chesed* is having a whole palette of stitching ideas and no structure to implement them. Pure *gevorah* is having the needle in your hand yet being unable to make a single stitch. *Chesed* is the right arm and *gevorah* is the left. Together they are the giving and receiving that work as one to allow full engagement in the stitching process.

In creation, *chesed* was created on the first day and *gevorah* on the second. The separation of sea and dry land was created on the third. Plants, also created on the third day, demonstrate the world of controlled aesthetic growth, the *chesed/gevorah* balance.

Evil occurs when *gevorah* rules without *chesed*. I arrived at a deep understanding of this last spring when I joined a local group of teachers to visit the Nazi concentration camps in Poland. I saw rows of children's mug shots in the hallway, a series of rooms each dedicated to a floor-to-ceiling pile of discarded shoes, suitcases, eyeglasses, cooking utensils, and clothing, and additional displays showing mountains of human hair and teeth. I was particularly struck by the prisoners' uniforms, in the odd way that only a sewer would notice: the closures, hems, and fabric texture. As the quilter in the group, I organized and constructed a signature quilt for all the trip participants that now hangs in our sponsoring institution.

In total *gevorah*, a person does not care about others and finds it impossible to love someone else or to be loved in return. That person becomes withdrawn, totally self-contained, and lost from humanity. This is what occurred on a spiritual level during the Holocaust and unfortunately it is easy to access while looking at the evidence of the atrocities that occurred during World War II in Europe.

The Twelve Steps

I am a huge fan of twelve-step programs. They offer us so much self-contained and self-generated wisdom and guidance. The original program was created for alcoholics. Since the founding of Alcoholics Anonymous (AA) by Bill W. in 1935, many other programs have adapted AA's original steps to their own addictions. These programs include such groups as Al-Anon/Alateen, Overeaters Anonymous, Gamblers Anonymous, and Narcotics Anonymous. Each follows its own modified version of the twelve steps.

The most widely recognized singular characteristic of any twelve-step program is the requirement that members admit that they have a problem. Participants share their experiences, challenges, successes, and failures and provide peer support for each other. The program of action, called The Twelve Steps, allows for change. Members select a sponsor, someone further on the path with some experience, to help them through the process.

My most successful experience with a twelve-step program is my artist group. We began meeting in 1997 and still continue to this day. Our addiction is one of self-limits and self-censorship. We follow the twelve steps to help unleash our creativity. Each of us can report great success with our method. We have made ourselves available for opportunities that had previously eluded us. For one exercise, we each created a pie chart of our lives with six sections: spirituality, exercise, play, work, friends, and romance/adventure. We filled in each section according to the level of activity in our lives for that category. I discovered I couldn't even place a dot in my romance/adventure section. That opened me to the idea of romance, and soon after I fell in love. Seeing the missing elements and being open to the possibilities allows the universe to bring exciting events into our lives.

I recommend checking out the twelve steps listed with any of the twelve-step programs. Use the step program for your own personal blockage or addiction and feel its power. The success of the twelve-step program is in the belief that we must let go of personal willpower and instead rely on a higher power. This program can work for atheists and agnostics by acknowledging the group itself as the higher power.

Achieving Wellness for a Healthy Self

Mind, body, spirit, and relationships all come together to form the state of wellness. Achieving a state of wellness means living a higher quality of life and experiencing a peace that goes beyond what material wealth or outside situations can offer. A state of wellness is priceless. It is available to each of us regardless of our circumstance. Wellness cannot be received externally. It comes as wealth from within. Wellness allows us to leave anxiety, drama, and disease behind and connects us with the wealth of inner peace. For lovers of fiber, wellness includes a tactile aesthetic—being surrounded by the warmth of fuzzy, soft, and cuddly textures.

Everything starts with the *aleph,* the breath. Take a moment and try this: Place the tip of your tongue against the inside of your front teeth. Exhale completely through your mouth. Inhale deeply through your nose with your mouth closed. Feel the air go all the way down to the bottom of your belly. Hold it for a couple of seconds. Exhale slowly through your mouth. Repeat this in-and-out breathing seven times.

I learned this breathing through meditation, but find it useful in all kinds of situations. This breathing slows us down so that we are fully with ourselves and in the moment. Breath is a great first step to wellness.

Achieving peace of mind together with superior mind-body health is complex. Our daily lives are packed with family, work, and community responsibilities. We are continuously juggling too many actions and too many things. Our days are difficult and sometimes even unbearable with all the worry and fear we carry. Fear and worry prevent us from living fully and happily in the moment. Reducing worry requires a change in how we view and react to situations. Worrying over things in the future wastes our present lives. Anxieties and fears and the resulting worry linger until we take action. We must work to discard the anxieties and fears that are not useful and change our focus to good and pleasant things in our lives that will help us maintain a peaceful and contented state of mind. Our goal is a stress-free life filled with contentment.

Our minds are sacred enclosures. Nothing harmful can enter without our permission. Acquiring knowledge, completing tasks, having pleasant experiences, and using kind conduct and words are actions that can help us. A practical solution is to slow down and limit our commitments. Take time to smell the flowers, and also to touch the cloth.

In the physical realm, we have one prime responsibility: to love and care for our bodies. It's all that we've got. We know how to take care of that body: good nutrition, regular exercise, comfortable clothing, preventive measures, natural remedies, restful sleep, and relaxation. Once we start quilting, it's hard to stop, but it's important to take breaks and do something physical. Try stretching, walking, lifting weights, or even stitching while sitting on one of those great balance balls.

Spirit, the wellspring of wisdom, courage, and strength, is our source of health and growth that connects us with all living things. Keep in touch with your divine connection, separate from your personal beliefs. Quilt making is potentially a great vehicle of access.

We want relationships that support our work and life purpose and fulfill us while being free of ego and complication. The biggest obstacle is our inability to put ourselves first, our codependency with others. The term *codependency* describes the responses and behaviors that individuals develop living with an alcoholic or other substance abuser. These are dysfunctional patterns that work around and even support the other's addictive behavior. Relationships with drug abusers cause us great emotional pain and stress, and so we use codependency as a survival technique.

Our tendency is to act against our own will or desires by trying desperately to satisfy others. Quilt makers tend to be caregivers, a role that can encourage codependent behavior. Caregivers can get involved with people who are unreliable, emotionally unavailable, and needy. We resort to compromising behaviors without addressing our own needs or desires. We set ourselves up for continual nonfulfillment. We may continue to behave dysfunctionally even when we encounter someone with healthy boundaries. Codependent coping behavior can prevent us from forming new relationships with people who have healthy behaviors and coping skills.

Symptoms of codependency include controlling behavior, distrust, perfectionism, avoidance of feelings, and intimacy problems. We are exhibiting codependent behavior if we are feeling consistently unfulfilled in relationships or we tend to be indirect and don't assert ourselves when we have a need or if we find ourselves too serious and not able to be playful.

Our life lessons will not disappear. Rather, they will keep presenting themselves until we learn them. Change starts through the bold expression of our needs, our likes, and our dislikes. We must acquire good communication skills, including listening and assertiveness, setting boundaries and using "I" messages to speak our feelings.

We can't depend on the other person to change. We can only change ourselves. Communication is the healthy way of stating our dislikes and getting our needs met. Communication involves practice and unlearning the old familiar automatic patterns. Unhealthy tactics we use to cope include nonverbal passive-aggression, isolation, acting out, verbal aggression, passive-placation, numbing, a don't-care attitude, and depression. We can begin by listening to others with empathic responses restating what was said without solutions, embellishment, or talking about ourselves. Another major part of our recovery is to let go and have fun. Our quilting is an opportunity to let go, create, and feel joy, the ultimate in self-nurture. Develop fierce and tender concern for yourself, and it will overflow to all those around you.

I will end with two pieces of very practical advice. There is nothing more important than a good night's sleep, allowing a fresh start each and every morning. Each day is a turning point, a new opportunity to put the right effort into achieving happiness. The second is the power of sound. Good listening is one thing that really affects my mood and helps me with my feelings. While working, I use unabridged audio books, instructional/inspirational CDs, and an assortment of classical and contemporary music.

Ultimately it is a personal decision what we incorporate and how we customize our personal needs and our individual journey. Allow quilting to support your life in an ambience of contentment.

Contemporary Quilting

Whenever someone comes to visit me, I inevitably get out some of my contemporary quilt books. These full-color catalogues document the larger, more innovative art quilt exhibitions occurring internationally. The art quilt movement is thriving, and it is truly inspirational to see the range of expression. Art quilts are looking more and more like paintings. There are no size limits at either end of the spectrum. They use a variety of materials and a multitude of techniques. Surface techniques include dyeing, drawing, monoprinting, digital printing, stamping, airbrushing, and heat transfers. Fabric-manipulation techniques include pleating, tearing, hand stitching, hand and machine appliqué, reverse appliqué, embroidery, collage, and machine quilting. It is possible and even likely to see uncut threads, exposed seams, and even wrong sides becoming right sides. Materials include cotton, silk, wool, velvet, satin, felt, paper, nylon net, plastic, beads, buttons, bows, disposable face cloths, metals, wires, candy wrappers, paper clips, and matchsticks. Themes are also as variable as the artists, ranging from personal, to political, to spiritual, and beyond. The quilt is constantly being redefined, and the definition of fiber expanded.

Quilt artists engage in the age-old question of art versus craft. We strive to be taken as serious fine artists who are using a craft medium. It is quite an uphill battle, mainly because we are so reluctant to take on the title of artist without somehow proving ourselves. From the art side, it is interesting to go to an international art exhibition and see the number of fine artists who have chosen fiber as their medium. This labeling and self-identity is a sad state of affairs. Avoid the dilemma. Because we are interested in quilting as a process to elevate spirit, we have to look at everything, everywhere, for approaches to our craft that appeal and are applicable to us.

There have always been many men working in the quilt medium. I did some informal research on the subject, and I found that there is absolutely no difference between the men and the women doing this work. Love of fiber and textile has nothing to do with gender. If there are a limited number of men in the field, it stems from a societal problem where men are not encouraged to be in touch with their softer side. So, male readers, my special advice to you is to take particular care of yourself, just as we women must do. Don't be afraid to discover and explore within. Your actions will have universal benefits for all of us.

QUILTING CARRY-ALL BAG

This is a trendy yet simple cloth sack made out of old jeans. This is one of those projects that works like a magic trick to amaze relatives and win friends. The size of the overalls will determine the size of your finished bag, so consider this as you approach the project.

Supplies

> 1 pair of overalls
>
> Velcro strip, long enough to go across the opening of your bag
>
> Sewing thread
>
> Fabric scissors

Directions

1. Cut open the inside seam of the pant legs along the seam edge. Cut off the legs of the jeans right above the crotch.

2. Cut off the upper portion of the overalls $\frac{1}{4}$ inch above the waistline in both the front and the back. Put this section aside to use as the straps and outside pockets of the bag.

3. Lay out the pant legs wrong sides together with the edges of the hem bottoms matching. Use the remaining center section of the overalls, the part with the side and back pockets, as a pattern to cut the leg pieces. The leg pieces will be the outside of the bag. Piece as necessary. The center pocket piece will be the inside lining of the bag.

4. Unfasten the buckles of the overalls. We will refasten them at the end to serve as the handles of the bag. Stitch the top portions of the overalls to each pant leg, keeping the hem edges as the top of the bag. The pocket portion of the overalls will be the

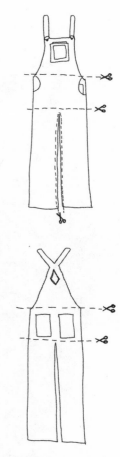

Cut the overalls as shown above.

front of the bag, and the back buckle portion of the back of the overalls will be the back of the bag.

5. Stitch the pant legs right sides together on three sides, leaving the hem edge as the top opening of the back. Turn right side to outside. This is the outside of the bag.

6. Turn the central portion of the overalls wrong sides out, and stitch the bottom closed. Depending on where you cut off the pant legs, you may have to overlap the crotch edges to make the material lie flat. This is the inside of the bag.

7. Place the central portion inside the pant-leg portion, wrong sides together. Pin the top, folding under the raw edge $1/4$ inch on inside pocket portion. The hem edge on the pants portion is a finished edge. Pin, baste, or stitch as needed to stabilize the piece to attach the Velcro.

8. Attach the Velcro all along the inside of the top edge of the bag, being careful not to include the strap portions.

9. Buckle up the overalls to complete the construction.

Variations

- Invite friends over for an afternoon of transforming old jeans into unique carry-alls for each other. Use the frayed seams of the jeans as handles and maintain pockets as practical embellishments.

- Felt an old wool sweater by washing it in hot water with detergent, and use that as the material for a new bag.

- Piece a patchwork outside for your bag and line it with the top of a pair of black dress pants.

- Offer to do a bag workshop for your local group members. Have them bring their favorite bags to use as inspiration and design possibilities.

BEHOLDING BEAUTY

Wearable Quilts

Tiferet: *the ideal balance of justice and mercy
needed to operate the universe.*

There are many reasons I don't particularly like to make clothing. I began in the fiber art world by learning clothing construction in my high school home economics class. I would spend hours selecting the fabric and the pattern and cutting, pinning, fitting, sewing, and pressing only to find more often than not that the result wasn't even close to my original vision. The completed garment was consistently lacking in one area or another: fit, aesthetics, technique, comfort, or cost. This was in the early sixties. Then along came the discount clothing stores, where I was able to successfully fill my closet with ready-made fashions that met all of my criteria. The process took less time, it was its own breed of fun, and I was spending less money. There was another benefit: It was stimulating to see the variety of approaches to clothing construction and materials in these clothing stores. What I observed spurred my creative endeavors with fiber in complementary directions, such as crafting bed quilts and wall hangings.

We have a store here in Pittsburgh that really can't be beat as far as the fashion discount-house experience goes. I travel there time and time again for the thrill of discovery. It's my favorite outing with my daughters. It works best when I arrive without needs or expectations. My goal is to get a bargain garment that is flattering on my body. This is simple, enormous fun, and I am always successful.

Nevertheless, having made the impressive argument for not wanting to spend my quilting time sewing garments, I recently had two remarkable clothing construction experiences. Throughout both experiences, I found myself at my machine giddy with glee, grateful for the good fortune to be given these opportunities and very pleased with the resulting products.

My first clothing construction experience began in the early seventies when I was a member of a consciousness-raising group. Our group was one of hundreds existing simultaneously in many parts of the world. We gathered weekly in each other's homes to study topics such as childhood, jobs, relationships, and sexuality. The general idea was to get to the root problems in society by studying our own situations as women. Our personal experiences were the source of everything we needed to know and understand. Occasionally we brought in outside reading, but our starting and ending points for discussion were our actual experiences. This process brought us into the full reality of our own lives. It was an essential part of the overall feminist strategy of the woman's movement to arrive at personal truth and then convert it into a means for action and organizing. This consciousness-raising involved us in both theory and strategy. We immediately became the experts of our own reality and what we might want or need to do to change it.

Looking back, it was amazing how much insight and understanding we derived from the simple honest pooling of experience. We were women interested in discerning and devising new theories and actions that reflected our authentic experience and feelings. Through our exchanges of personal feelings and experiences we developed deep long-lasting and supportive friendships.

The first garment I created was for a friend from that original consciousness-raising group. At the time of the group, we both lived in Philadelphia. Now she lives in Washington, D.C. Over the years we have maintained our friendship through visits, life-cycle events, vacations, telephone, and e-mail. On a recent Sunday morning brunch in her backyard, we acknowledged how the system of our group, developed so many years before, helped our friendship endure. We had adhered to the long-established consciousness-raising method of communication that made it possible to get right to each of our hearts whenever we came together.

Some twelve or so years ago, I made her and her husband a wonderful contemporary bed quilt for their queen-size bed. Last spring, she sent me the quilt, wondering if it could be salvaged. They had made good use of it and still adored it. However, several of the fabrics that formed part of the patchwork top were shredded. It required too much repair work to make a recovery practical. Instead, I made them a new updated quilt of a similar design and contemporary fabrics. She loved the replacement quilt. While we were together, I mentioned that I still had the old quilt and that if she was interested, I could cut out some of the nicer sections of it and make her a wearable quilt. She was enthusiastic about having the older quilt transformed and making it part of her life once again.

I was hesitating over the process, fearful of making an irretrievable cutting mistake, when the second opportunity presented itself. This came through the partner of my beloved's father, a woman in her seventies. I met her when we visited them in Idaho. I felt a strong and immediate bond with this couple. Their relationship was wonderfully warm and complementary and functioned admirably. It was obvious that they cared greatly for each other and were particularly considerate of each other. It was heartwarming. We had a great time getting to know each other—sharing time, food, adventures, and ideas. They had both lost their spouses after many years of marriage.

Knowing I loved textiles, she rummaged through her storage boxes and pulled out a large collection of hand-batik cloth. There were yards of fabric and several skirts and dresses. The items had been in storage for a long time. It was clear that these fabrics represented precious memories for her. She loved them, but had no current use for them, and so had kept them stowed away.

Wanting to repay her hospitality with the best possible gift, I offered to take the textiles and transform them. She struggled long and hard with my offer. While she loved the idea and longed to get some actual use out of the cloth, she was nervous and hesitant about the process and product. The materials were too precious. Was it right to alter any of them? What if something went amiss? After much debate, we settled on a stunning hand-batik dress in black, red, tan, and white. It was too small for her, and she hadn't worn it in over twenty years. I had her permission to transform that one piece of cloth into an article of clothing for her to wear.

The two projects lay waiting on my worktable: two very distinctive women—one whom I had known for years, the other for just a week—and two very singular kinds of cloth: a worn-out patchwork quilt and a fitted Indonesian batik dress. The hardest part in each instance was making the first cut. The owners of the cloth had entrusted me with material that was enormously precious to them. Once I made a cut in the fabric, there would be no turning back.

In the end I made the same garment for both: a short poncho-type jacket with a front-tie closure. I made notes and measurements from garments and photographs I had on hand. I began slowly, cutting out first the backs, then the fronts, and last of all the sleeves. By the time I found myself at the sewing machine attaching the pieces, I was reasonably confident I had succeeded.

Analyzing the experience brings a larger symbolism to the story. My long-standing friend adored her new jacket because when she put it on, she came into contact with our spirits and the strong bond between us. The older woman expressed gratitude for both her new friendship with me and how wearing the new piece of clothing helped her incorporate some of her past life experience into her present. She wore her jacket to the symphony and felt warm, comforted, and loved. I learned something about the eternal nature of time through its endless mixing of the old and the new. The memories themselves have value. Yet in this instance, it's not only the memories themselves that matter, it's is how we inte-grate the past into the present and beyond. It's where real action and the resulting satisfaction arise. Each of us involved in this adventure learned a unique lesson about embracing and integrating the old with the new. Both women had a transformative experience derived from an obsolete textile turned into a source of owner's pride. My old friend and my new friend were thrilled with the results, and I remained gleeful with the creation process.

But making clothing for myself is still an issue for me because it's tied into the much larger issue of covering my body and my self-image in general. It is hard to admit, but I still look in the mirror every day and wonder who I am. Not knowing who I am makes me unclear about what kind of dress I like and will be comfortable wearing.

It's quite amusing to think back over all the different periods of my life and the fashion statements that accompa-nied each. When I was in high school, weighing less than a hundred pounds, I never ever considered wearing a pair of pants. I thought it accentuated my pear shape. As a freshman in college, I was required to wear skirts to class, and I acqui-esced, sticking to the basic collegiate look of the day. When the Vietnam antiwar movement hit, my closet was revamped, and all I owned were jeans and T-shirts. As a young mother, comfort became the key to success, which meant wearing simple pants and tops. In my forties, I went through a long period of only wearing black, trying desperately not to see myself or be seen.

Throughout each of these periods, getting dressed for an occasion represented the biggest struggle. I have trouble keeping up to date with the latest fashions. It took an over-whelming effort to create a total look. It was just too chal-lenging to put together a head-to-toe outfit, including shoes, stockings, jewelry, and accessories, and have it work. Why was that? What was my problem? What did all of this mean? Bottom line, I never felt as if any of my clothing choices truly represented the authentic me. The times and fashions changed, but even to this day, hints of the issue remain. One of the things I have always loved about being an artist is how I can make the work and then separate myself from it by hanging it on my wall away from my person—a simple way to avoid the self-image dilemma.

I continue to come to terms with my body, my image, and my authentic self, struggling to integrate them into one fluid person. It is a process of accepting who I am and who I am becoming, day in and day out. Experiences like those of making my friends' jackets help me pinpoint how and why clothing is meaningful and more than just a look or a fashion. As I grow into my skin and become more comfortable with myself, there are actually some days I feel so compatible with my clothing choices that I am reluctant to remove the garments for sleep. In those instances, I have accepted who I am and know the choice allows my heart to shine through with the appearance and the style.

Tiferet: Gateway to the Divine

Tiferet is associated with the power to reconcile conflicting inclinations. It is the real self, being able to stand at the crossroads with compassion. It is often called the attribute of mercy, as it takes great mercy and great compassion to stand in the middle of a conflict and just let it be, to accept it as it is. *Tiferet* corresponds to the heart, to the very core of our beings. The beauty of *tiferet* manifests itself through the elegant blend of emotive gestures implicit within it.

Tiferet, or beauty, is attained by contrasting elements, allowing them to play with each other. If we look at color, beauty does not eliminate the contrasts turning everything to a dull brown or gray, rather beauty combines both black and white and all the colors into a picture of depth. Contrasts come together into an integrated whole. I am with the *tiferet* in me as I view myself in the mirror and allow and accept what I see as the physical me, just as I am, with no need to change and alter, only to accept and even enjoy and be grateful.

The goal of *tiferet* is for us to develop our greatest potential as human beings. On the Tree of Life it is in a triad with *chesed,* or lovingkindness, and *gevurah,* or strength. As a part of the triad, *tiferet* will help us balance open-heartedness with our need for limits and boundaries. In addition, being in the center of the tree, it is the attribute most connected to each of the others and in that way accepts all our aspects as they are. In my case, a healthy combination of these attributes means combining my desire to dress in the fashion of the times with my need to wear clothing that accentuates my physical being and is at the same time comfortable and fun to wear.

The Components of the Human Soul

Let's take a moment to look at the human spirit. In Kabbalah each of us has a spiritual component, that spark of life that is a fragment of divine light. Each is unique and special with its particular action, function, and path. Each of our spirits has five interconnected levels. These components can be thought of as concentric circles, each one larger and encompassing the ones before it.

The first is *nefesh,* the dense central core of our human manifestation. *Nefesh* is located energetically in the lower part of the body. It is the living force that enlivens the body and gives us our appetite for life. Some call it the animal soul because it is associated with our physical selves.

Ruach is the emotional and psychological component of human spirit. *Ruach* means breath. *Ruach* is located in the heart energy field and is the part of our soul that responds to music, dance, and the visual arts.

The third layer is *neshamah. Neshamah* is our higher beliefs, our capacity to think, imagine, and be inspired by more intellectual pursuits, such as philosophy and mathematics. It translates into our lives as meaning, attitude, and our personal politics. Energetically, *neshamah* is located near the third eye somewhere in the forehead area. As we do spiritual work, we are engaging with any or all of these levels of spirit.

Chayah, the fourth level, is our divine self, which agreed to this life and our specific work. *Chayah* corresponds to the action of the forces of the attributes in this world. *Yechida* is the last and is our timeless self and the impersonal aspect of the great totality. *Yechida* is the great oneness within which our individual self is no longer separate, the point of contact between the human spirit and the very essence of the Divine. *Yechida* simply exists and is free to realize its true nature when you attend to the other levels of soul within your field of awareness. Neither *chayah* nor *yechida* are generally accessible to us as humans in this world.

Our spirit is the source of our capacity to think, imagine, dream, and contemplate. All these spirit parts come together to form our unique self, integrated and functioning with the divine attributes, bringing everything into a oneness of action in this moment in this universe.

The kabbalists use the term *garments* in many of their texts. This refers to the layers that cover the divine light so that it can be seen and understood at a human level. When we look directly at the sun, we are blinded by the light and can't see anything. The universes, the *sefirot* or attributes, and the levels of spirit are the many layers or garments that serve to both conceal and reveal the power of the light. For all its common points and resemblance to others, each spirit is unique unto itself and justifies its separate existence. This is the meeting place of the Divine and human, each seeking the other to comprehend the potential of human existence.

As we put together all these pieces, we become aware of a vast arc curving from the Divine to each of us. This corresponds to the question: Where do I come from? At the same time there is a line curving from each of us to the Divine, which corresponds to the question: Where am I going? Within this circle are all the levels of human nature. Each human has a unique path and special lines of individual direction and expression. These are not simply random points in reality but are expressions of our individual person-alities and the shape of our individual spirits. All spirits flow in and out from the Divine. All similarly aspire to reach out and grow and eventually to return to the Divine. In this way we delineate ourselves from both the outside in and the inside out.

Prayer at the Crossroads of Compassion

Tiferet gives us a vehicle to send love, truth, and beauty into the world. This important job begins with sending love, truth, and beauty to ourselves. I must have a compassionate open-hearted attitude about myself and my quandary about clothing. I understand that as I come more and more into my true nature, my authentic self, clothing choices will follow. At that point, my dress becomes an extension of my spirit. It certainly sounds easy and uncomplicated, yet we know from experience that this is a long arduous path. The first question is how might we open our hearts, and then other questions will follow. Once we make that opening, crack the surface, we will have to work with the new territory—massage it, water it, feed it and tend it, learning to grow into and with our open-hearted nature.

Fortunately, we have a technique for opening the heart. This is a communication system with the Divine called prayer. It is an active searching and exploring with the Divine. Through this investigation, we will come to many understandings of our own particular beings and our roles here in this world. Without prayer, it is easy for our emotions to enclose us, giving rise to negativity and a brittle heart that becomes more and more closed, hoping desperately to pro-tect itself from hurt and pain. Prayer allows for movement, opening, and the opportunity to alter our view, to see and engage in new and different systems of experience. It becomes a process of expansion, becoming a bigger and big-ger container for all our experiences, where joy can exist alongside the pain and all is part of the Divine and our con-nection to the oneness.

All religions have their own unique formal prayers and meditations. For the quilting experience, I am talking about individual prayer, using personal language to speak directly from our hearts to the Divine. This prayer will be an example of true beauty because it will be honest and direct. Speak what is on your mind. Start right where you are, and let the words develop as they may. At first, this might prove difficult. Look at all the years it took me to figure out what to wear. But like anything, it is a process. As we keep going, continuing our honest words, we begin to hear answers. We understand that the Divine listens, not from some mystical state of perfection, but from being with us just as we are in each moment, with our aspirations, concerns, and quandaries. Eventually, we hear all: the Divine, the universe, and our true selves in everything we do and all that we are and desire to become.

The heart is the seat of consciousness. By quieting the heart, we create inner peace that soothes the soul and calms the mind. Quieting the heart is the process of cultivating intentionality, the ability to concentrate wholeheartedly on a single task or object, which is a critical element of prayer. We seek to reduce the cacophonous voice of the self and thereby open an avenue through which the transcendent dimension of the Divine, the oneness, can communicate with the internal dimension of the Divine, the individual I, and unite them.

Prayer Garments

Different kinds of prayer garments help us to continually recommit ourselves to our mission. The scapular in Roman Catholicism forms an important part of the habit of the monastic orders; it is made up of two small squares of wool fabric, sometimes bearing images, suspended by cords over the chest and back. Both male and female orders and religious congregations have adopted the scapular from the monastic orders. An example is the brown scapular adapted from the scapular of the Carmelite Order. People who wear it practice a special devotion to Mary. The scapular reminds them of Mary's promise to help those consecrated to her obtain the grace of final perseverance.

Mormons, members of the Church of Jesus Christ of Latter-day Saints, wear special underwear known as a temple garment. This is a white garment worn close to the skin and inscribed with secret markings, serving as a testimony of devotion and a reminder of certain temple rites. A Mormon receives his or her first temple garment after undergoing the temple endowments ceremony, usually when he or she gets married or goes on a religious mission. The garment, worn day and night, serves as a continuous reminder of the sacred covenants. It is a symbol of modest dress and living.

In addition to a robe, the garment of a Zen Buddhist practitioner is a *raksu*. This is an abbreviated form of the *kesa,* the patched one-piece robe that is identified with Shakyamuni Buddha himself. Individuals make their own *raksu* and have their Buddhist name inscribed on the underside by their teacher.

In Judaism there is the *tallit,* a garment like a shawl with four sets of threads tied into knots at the corners. The knots remind the wearer of the 613 commandments from the laws of the Torah.

Some nuns have habits, some priests have white collars, and some monks shave their heads and wear robes. These examples show us the wide variety of spiritual garments and encourage our personal pursuit of making something that is uniquely appropriate for our individual spiritual expression.

Getting dressed without giving it much thought is clothing. Dressing for effect is costuming. Covering oneself with a spiritual garment is locating the beauty within ourselves and connecting it to the Divine.

The Patchwork Shawl project is an opportunity to make your own garment of spirit. This simple shawl can be used for formal prayer, but also at other times, to wrap you in awareness, hope, aspiration, acknowledgment, and wonder.

We will construct a long rectangle made of half-square triangles. Triangles represent how things often appear in threes. In Kabbalah, we talk of the three mothers, the three Hebrew letters at the foundation of the language. It is said that from them spring the three fathers and all things in this world, including the division of male and female. In another set of threes, the heavens were from fire, the earth from water, and the spirit from air. In Christian tradition, the number three symbolizes the Trinity of the Father (or Creator), the Son (or Redeemer), and the Holy Ghost (or Sustainer). Buddhists have the Three Jewels: the Buddha, or the enlightened one, the *dharma,* or the teachings, and the *sangha,* or the community of followers. In most faiths we have another set of three: the body, the mind, and the spirit.

PATCHWORK SHAWL

For the shawl shown here, instead of using the new fabric, I used twenty-five men's ties and five men's shirts that I cut and pieced to fulfill the fabric requirements. At the completion of the garment, take some time to open your heart to the Divine and write a prayer on the inside of your shawl. Sign and date it.

Supplies

> 2 yards backing fabric
>
> 2½ yards assorted fabrics for patchwork
>
> Sewing thread that matches backing
>
> Permanent ink marker

Directions

1. Piece the backing fabric as necessary to form one large rectangle at least 26 inches by 75 inches for the shawl and two 26-inch-by-15-inch rectangles for the pockets at the edge of the shawl.

2. Cut at least 105 5-inch squares from your assortment of fabrics. Cut each of those along the diagonal until you have at least 210 triangles. As possible, layer fabrics to speed the cutting process. With a good rotary cutter it is possible to cut as many as 12 layers at one time. First cut 5-inch strips, and then layer the strips: cut them into squares, and then into triangles.

3. Randomly mixing the fabrics, piece the triangles to form 105 4½-inch squares. These are called half-square triangles.

4. Chain piece the half-square triangles into rows, 5 across and 17 down for the front and 2 pieces 5 across and 2 down for the pockets.

5. Center the rows of half-square triangles onto the backing, wrong sides together. Stitch rows to each

other and the backing at the same time, using the quilt-as-you-go method (see p. 15).

6. Trim the excess backing to 1½ inches larger than the patchwork on all four sides.

7. Line the pocket pieces right sides together by placing the pocket patchwork and the backing rectangle wrong sides together. Leave an extra edge of backing 1½ inches at the top of the pocket. Trim the other three sides even with the patchwork.

8. Finish the top edge of the pocket by turning in the raw edge of the backing to meet the patchwork, and then again to enclose all the raw edges in the binding. Stitch through all the layers at the folded edge of the binding.

9. Place one pocket at each edge of the shawl. Do the double fold of the backing by turning in the raw edge of the backing to meet the patchwork, and then again to enclose all the raw edges in the binding. Stitch through all the layers at the folded edge of the binding, including the unfinished pocket edges at either end.

10. Stitch down the middle line of patchwork of each pocket end to form two pockets on either side.

11. Find a quiet place and time to talk to the Divine about the content and wording of your prayer. Using a permanent ink marker, write your prayer on the lining of your shawl. Sign and date the writing.

Variations

- Add decorative elements to your shawl such as buttons and ties.

- Remake the shawl as a gift for a friend.

- Change the pattern shape into a larger shawl or a poncho for a special occasion.

- Adapt the patchwork piecing to create a garment using a traditional store-bought pattern.

- Make another prayer shawl with a different purpose and a new prayer.

A PICTURE OF PLACE AND TIME

Appliqué Quilt

Hod: *empathy, splendor, glory, majesty.*

I live in Pittsburgh, a city that operates like a small town. We have many modest insular neighborhoods, naturally divided by rivers, bridges, hills, and valleys. I'm pretty typical of the homegrown variety in that most of my life has taken place working and playing within the same five-mile radius. In the day-to-day operations of my life, it is common for me to intersect with someone from my past. Even when one of us 'burghers moves away, we still have a strong identity with the town. I can't really explain it except to acknowledge our peculiar affinity for each other and our place.

I raised my children in a traditional home in a family-oriented neighborhood. It had the feel of the suburbs even though it was within the city limits. Our street was a cul-de-sac, a half circle connected to another lightly traveled residential street. That street connected to a large intersection with major public transportation that provided access to any part in the city. When I remember our street, I visualize my children as youngsters out in the road riding bicycles and playing games, while we, the watchful parents, stood near the central island, swapping stories, information, and gossip.

The house where I raised my family began as a simple, compact red-brick house. In my younger days, all I wanted was a big old fixer-upper with hardwood trim and a grand staircase, something that wasn't realistic given our budgetary constraints. My mom found our starter home for us, and she was clear in her instruction. This was an adequate and affordable house in a good neighborhood. It had creative potential, and over time we

113

could make it into whatever we wanted. We did just that. There were two additions, beautiful renovations, and constant improvements. By the time we had finished putting our stamp on it, our homestead was a special place to grow, live, work, and entertain.

The first addition contained the all-important sewing studio. We built it on the second level of a two-story space so I could be in constant voice contact with the children, who mostly occupied the family room on the lower level. It was a funny thing: because the children didn't actually see me, they often forgot about me, yet I could intervene as needed while continuing my work at the sewing machine. I had two techniques to keep at the work that are worth sharing here. The first is that I refused to stop in the middle of an operation, and everyone knew that. No matter the request, each knew there would be a delay before I left the studio for the necessary action. The other was that every night after I put the kids to bed, I took a brief nap and then did the bulk of my creative work in the beautiful silence of late-night privacy. The second addition was a larger kitchen and eating area to accommodate a growing family. As always, each addition created walls and spaces to display the ever-expanding quilt collection.

The one thing missing from this family haven was a view. Pittsburgh is a town at the edge of the Allegheny Mountains. It affords magnificent views. Unfortunately, we lived in a valley near the Allegheny River with no view access. That deficiency created a continual kind of daydreaming for me about another place that included the view for which Pittsburgh was famous.

One day I saw an ad in the paper for townhouses on one of the mountains near downtown. It claimed to have the beautiful views of my longing at an affordable price. I couldn't resist a Sunday joy ride to check it out. My youngest was a senior in high school, and I had promised she would graduate from her childhood home. Still I couldn't resist this little indulgence to my daydreaming, assuming it was harmless with little substance.

The townhouses were indeed reasonable and offered spectacular views. But six levels of living meant lots of stairs, and the views weren't enough to entice an exit from our treasured family home. The realtor suggested another stop that I might enjoy for my Sunday browse. It was a renovated loft building on Pittsburgh's southside, a building that had been the bottling plant of the Duquesne Brewery. Loft buildings are few and far between here, so it was an opportunity to see something a little different and artsy. Part of my daydreaming did include that kind of open artistic space. On our way home, we stopped off to take a look.

The outside was anything but captivating—a light industrial neighborhood with patchy streets, trucks, and an active train track right at its rear. This introduction left me unprepared for the inside. I walked into the model and was transfixed. The space itself was captivating, and when I stepped onto a private porch and saw the University of Pittsburgh's Cathedral of Learning, I knew this was the location of my dreams. It certainly was enough of a view for me, and the space was magnificent. Fifteen-foot ceilings, large windows, exposed steel beams, and the potential to building out the space in any way my imagination might take me.

I spent the next six weeks asking myself whether I could make this kind of a move. The space seemed so right for me; it was affordable, captivating, and I felt a longing to be there. Yet, crossing the river felt like moving to Chicago. How would it be to leave my five-mile comfort zone? What about my promise to my children to remain in their childhood home? The debate with myself was driving me crazy, so I called upon my cousin, a realtor. My thought was to take her to see it, have her nix the idea, and that would be that. That was not what occurred. She loved the place, found it truly intriguing, and thought it a great option for me. Along with her seal of approval came oodles of advice about negotiating the sale of my house, getting the best deal on the loft, organizing the construction, and getting the children to buy into the idea. It all worked. I sold the house but we remained there until graduation. My youngest daughter's graduation party was an unqualified success, held in an under-construction loft complete with scaffolding, catered food, and a live jazz band.

The construction itself was harrowing, but having done renovation before, I was prepared for the onslaught of problems and adjustments. I knew that my virtue of patience would serve me well in the end. Moving to the loft is probably the single best thing I've ever done for my quilt-making self. The loft brought the creative forces down front and center. I had that wonderful workroom in our house, but it was up in a corner and off to the side. I had to make a special effort and expend some energy to head up there. In this loft everything is in easy reach—a couple of steps in any direction to the work area, to the computer, to the library, to the kitchen, and so on. There is a constant flow of action and movement releasing all kinds of opportunities. Projects abound, and it's stimulating no matter where one lands in the space. The open nature of the area fosters continual communication among its inhabitants and makes for increased contact with everything entering the area. Nothing works in isolation. I wake up every morning and go to sleep every night deeply grateful for the luxury of this special place to honor and take care of me.

The loft is an ample 2,700 square feet on two stories. That's a lot of air. The water pipes, heating ducts, and electrical wiring are all exposed. The floor is concrete, and the ceiling is steel beams and corrugated cement. Every section of wall is painted a different color. Over twenty colors of paint and more than thirty antique oriental rugs and quilts, too numerous to count, activate the space with an abundance of color. I haven't said very much about specific colors in our quilts, mainly because my color choices are always so variable that it's difficult to know what advice I might give that would be truly helpful.

Writing about the loft becomes an opportunity to tackle color and see what light we can shed on it.

Color as Covenant

Our most basic information about color comes from the Hebrew Bible and the story of Noah. The Divine tells Noah that the rainbow is a sign of the covenant. A covenant is a formal, solemn, and binding agreement. In the story a rainbow is used to represent divine light. Divine light is white light consisting of all colors. In a rainbow, the white light passes through a prism and is refracted and divided into many colors. Noah and his wife Na'amah are our universal ancestors. The collective covenant is for all of us, the descendents of Noah and Na'amah. This rainbow covenant applies to all of humankind in every place so that we function as a prism for the full spectrum of the Divine's radiant glory.

The covenant exists today as the Seven Laws of Noah. Their observance ensures a civilized and peaceful world. The first of the Seven Laws of Noah is the prohibition against idol worship. Idolatry denies the essence of religion by worshipping another deity besides the Creator. We are prohibited from serving or worshipping any created thing—no human being, angel, plant, or star, none of the four fundamental elements, earth, water, fire, and air, or anything formulated from them. Observing the prohibition against idol worship makes us aware of universal unity.

Blasphemy is the second law. This is the act of cursing the Creator or something of the creation. This is about right speech and not misusing the faculty of communication. Someone blasphemes because of an incomplete belief in the absolute oneness.

For the third law, we are prohibited from killing a human being. The fourth is the prohibition of illicit sexual relations, including certain relatives and another's spouse. Many issues, such as capital punishment, fall under these two laws, and in many cases, there are ongoing differences of opinions as to the truthful application of divine intent.

The fifth Noachian law is the prohibition of theft, and the sixth prohibits removing a limb of a living creature. Both are examples of human cruelty and selfishness.

The seventh law is the establishment of courts of justice that are responsible for the maintenance of the Seven Laws of Noah. Courts of law institute justice, truth, righteousness, and morality. A judge in the Noachian court system needs to have wisdom and humility, be a lover of truth, and be beloved by the citizens of the community with an impeccable reputation.

Through the faithful observance of the Seven Laws of Noah, we can fulfill our purpose for existence, to perfect this world and in doing so reveal the divine plan here and now in this universe. The Hebrew word for commandment is *mitzvah*; the plural is *mitzvot*. The Seven Laws of Noah are the mitzvot for all of us. The Seven Laws of Noah are a guaranteed world peace plan for humankind to live in harmony. The observance of these Seven Laws of Noah brings all of humanity to its ultimate redemption: a share in the *Olam Ha Ba,* or the world to come. *Olam Ha Ba* is a reference to the messianic age and a higher state of being. The rabbis compare this world to a lobby before entering *Olam Ha Ba.* We prepare ourselves in the lobby so that we may enter the banquet hall. *Olam Ha Ba* is determined by a merit system based on our actions. *Olam Ha Ba* is characterized by the peaceful co-existence of all people. Hatred, intolerance, and war will cease to exist, and the righteous of all nations will share in this world.

Hod: The Bigger Picture of Place

Chesed signifies unlimited lovingkindness. *Gevorah* is the limitation and concealment of lovingkindness. Both define qualities of giving. The next two *sefirot, netzach* and *hod,* define our ability to receive. *Netzach* and *hod* correspond to the fourth and fifth days of creation, when the sun, moon, and stars were created. Even though light was created on the first day, this light was infinite and too sublime to be of use in our finite world. On the fourth day, a finite, usable form of light was apportioned. On the fifth day, birds and sea creatures were created. These are the first recipients of divine benevolence and the first created beings able to fulfill the commandment to be fruitful and multiply.

Most often translated as splendor, *hod* is the persistence of holding on. It is finding that place and the comfort of being in the right place at the right time. Its partner *netzach*, most often translated as eternity, is our capacity for conquest and overcoming. The powers of prophecy and divine inspiration derive from *netzach* and *hod*. This is the territory for all kinds of big and small miracles.

Hod represents thoughts and *netzach* our feelings. Each influences the other, and so these two divine attributes are often explored together. We can use the little things like the simple longing for a special view to connect us to the larger picture of where we are and where we are going.

Spiritual Colors

Chakras provide another way to identify color in the spiritual realms. The word *chakra* is Sanskrit for wheel or disk and signifies one of seven basic energy centers in the body. Each of these centers correlates to major nerve ganglia branching forth from the spinal column. They are not physical entities in and of themselves, yet they have a strong effect on the body as they are a form of spiritual energy on our physical plane. The chakras correlate to levels of consciousness, archetypal elements, and developmental stages of life. They each have sounds, body functions, and colors.

The highest chakra, at the crown of the head, is located in the cerebral cortex and associated with shades of violet. This is the opening to the universe for understanding, the right to learn and the right to know. Here we have the ability to perceive, analyze, and assimilate information.

The third-eye chakra is found in the center of the forehead, a little above and between the eyes, and is associated with the color indigo. Here we use our intuition, perception, and imagination to access dreams and think symbolically.

The throat chakra is found at the front center of the neck and reflects two elements, our ability to communicate and our awareness of inner truth. Together, they reflect our ability to communicate our inner truth to others. The color is a bright blue.

The heart chakra, located in the chest area, is associated with the color green. It reflects our understanding of love, our ability to direct it toward and receive it from others and ourselves.

The solar plexus is next, located just below the rib cage and linked to the color yellow. This chakra reflects our sense of self, our identity, and how we view both of these. Traditionally, it is the point from which we act and is the seat of our personal will.

Below the solar plexus is the vital or emotional center that is the basis for feeling, located in the lower abdomen. A primary nerve ganglion comes out of the spine at that chakra point, about two inches below the navel. It can be found by following a line across the top of the hipbones to the center of the abdomen. Its normal color is orange.

The lowest root chakra reflects our security, trust, and our survival instinct. It is our connection to the physical body. Its normal color is red, and the easiest way to locate it is directly across the points of the hips at the base of the spine.

I learned about chakras and energy work as the result of a quilt commission. I was hired to create a donor recognition quilt for a local agency that used a rainbow for its logo. When I met with them, they were certain that they did not like the trite image of a rainbow and were looking to me for something new and different. I began a search among my friends exploring what they associated with rainbows, and that led me to the chakras and their color connections. Next I looked at quilt patterns and ideas that might lend themselves to a color spectrum and a gradual change in color. I came up with a log cabin variation made in triangles instead of squares. The triangles represent the three rivers of

Pittsburgh, and I arranged the colors to flow through a series of quilts that today hang throughout the agency's building.

There are also color associations for the *sefirot,* the Tree of Life. The mystics developed systems that used different senses as a means of elevating themselves closer to the Divine. The main reason for all these systems is to provide a ladder upon which we can climb to higher and higher spiritual levels. The problem with colors is that it is easy to take them literally as something we can see and use to describe the physical world. When we describe the *sefirot* with physical properties, we begin to think of them in physical rather than spiritual terms. The answer is to think of the colors allegorically, alluding to their functions and the results. Therefore in *keter,* the highest of the *sefirot,* the color is transparent pure white or colorless like glass, representing the closeness we feel in relation to the Divine when we are operating at that spiritual level. *Chochmah* is associated with the color sapphire blue that includes all colors. Going back to *chochmah* as the beginning place of receiving from the Divine, we can understand that it is like Noah receiving the entire rainbow of color. *Binah* is linked with yellow or gold, *da'at* is transparent, and *chesed* is silver with a bluish tinge. *Gevurah* is red, and *tiferet* is a light green or citron color. *Netzach* and *hod* are light pink and dark pink respectively. *Yesod* is a rainbow of hues, including blue, red, and yellow, and *malkhut* is a dark blue with purple tinge.

We all have tendencies toward certain colors. Our moods and our feelings affect our use of color. Are there colors you like? Why? Are there colors that you stay away from? Why? For example, my latest favorite color is lime green. I kept one quilt from my last show and that was its main color. I bought an all-weather shell jacket, and its main color was lime green. The apple green wall in the loft is one of my favorites. I did a little research on my attraction to lime green. In the chakra system, green provides us with a new place near the heart for action. It allows us to act from other than will or the self, and it is an indicator of surrender of self-will to the will of creation. Following the color indicators of green in this system helps me integrate my current interest in that hue with the spiritual process I undertook to write this book.

We are fortunate that our work of quilt making naturally puts us in touch with all kinds of color. With spiritual colors, we come to understand that we can take our experience one step further and use color proactively in our work. We can bring our awareness of color to access the divine aspects of our longing. That's exactly what happened for me with my rainbow commission. Before I did the research for the commission, I was having a terrible time with the color yellow. Becoming aware of my yellow disconnect, I decided to use energy work to figure out why. Through a variety of techniques, I discovered that my difficulty with yellow related to a disturbing event from my childhood. It was the death of my grandmother when I was nine. It was not a physical thing such as my grandmother making me eat yellow food or ruining my favorite yellow dress. It was that when she died I could not accept it, and I held that in my body in the chakra area associated with yellow. While working on the quilt and specifically the yellow section, I used this time to remember my grandmother, to thank her for the unconditional love she gave me, and to say goodbye to her in a way I was unable to do as a child. This is an example of using the allegorical nature of color in our work. If I am working on *hod*, trying to discover my place, I can draw upon the shades of pink and use them in my work, allowing them to increase my awareness of all the aspects associated with that divine attribute.

There is a lot of specific technical information on color and color combinations. There are color wheels made specifically for quilters. There are books and exercises of color theory for artists. The problem here is that we might be too literal and physical with the colors. When we combine colors with spirit, we are entering a whole different realm. I'm going to give you a good twelve-step slogan of advice: Keep it simple. Don't drive yourself crazy trying to figure out colors and color combinations. Quilting fabrics have a great depth of color these days. Go with what you are attracted to, and trust your eye. If there are some issues in your life that are troubling or some parts of your body that are in question, look up the colors associated with them and play with the color to see what happens. For myself, I go back to my personal philosophy—the more colors the merrier. Go for it. Mix and match and have fun.

A Working Home Environment

In the introduction I mentioned finding a corner to call your own. Now it's time to take the next step. The best possible environment is one where you can leave things in process, where you can be alone when you need it, and where you have adequate light and space to take to completion what you want to accomplish. Organization of materials is the key. It allows easy access to all your resources: a bookshelf, fabrics organized into color groups, notions organized and readily available—a place for everything and everything in its place.

Most projects begin concurrently as both an idea and a fabric selection. I use resource notebooks to brainstorm ideas. These are loose-leaf binders that I keep and update regularly on every topic imaginable. I have visual and article notebooks all arranged in categories, such as fiber, ceramics, the human figure, mysticism, and Zen. These are examples of my categories, but you will develop your own.

The next step is the pattern. In this project we will be making a full-size drawing. If it is traditional patchwork, I work on graph paper. That brings me to my projects notebooks. I keep an ongoing graph-paper spiral notebook with notes on every single item I make, including measurements, sources, client contact information, and step-by-step decisions. I refer back to these often for other projects. It's great to have an organized accessible record.

Once the pattern is decided, the cutting begins. For the most part, I try to do all of one step before going on to the next. It saves time. Sometimes it's not possible because the project is too big, or I need to see one finished section to decide about the next. So there are lots of exceptions and deviations, but for me time is money, and that's always my bottom line: What will produce the best results in the least amount of time?

Next is the construction: first the patchwork or appliqué, followed by any embellishments or embroideries, and then the quilting, and finally the binding and hanging devices and the signature. One general tip is to always leave your project set up and ready to begin the next step when you return to it.

Folk Art Quilts

Folk art is a broad category of living traditions that are recorded in the craft format by their participants. Art in the sense it is used here refers not to a class of object but rather to that aspect of any object that goes beyond the strictly utilitarian and which is intended to give pleasure to the maker and/or viewer. "Folk" refers to the object having been made by members of a specific cultural subgroup of the greater society. The folk artist can produce either for his or her own personal use or for export beyond the family to the community and larger society.

Folk arts are linked to the creation of all art forms, yet craft workers use traditions handed down through the generations and preserve the creative values of the tradition in a visual form. The folk arts are created within small communities and serve the purposes of those communities. They tend to be conservative as their tradition exerts a strong pull on the artists who create within certain well-understood boundaries. Folk arts reflect the specific aesthetic standards of the community within which they are created. Folk artists learn their skills within their communities, using methods that are sanctioned by that particular community. These artists learn through formal or informal apprenticeship or by working with and observing older relatives. A folk artist's work becomes a statement of the traditional roots of the individual. Traditional does not mean unchanged. It means that folk art has a history, an intuitive connection with the past.

APPLIQUÉ QUILT

For my appliqué quilt, I chose to document a tree that has special significance for me. This is the tree in the yard of my love's home. It has a magnificent presence. I view and interact with this tree in many contexts. I park my car under it. We have an outdoor fire beside it, feeding the fire with its worn-out limbs. We have had picnics, taken naps, and played games under this tree. It harbors fabulous birds and wondrous rodents. I have even raked its leaves. I can see it from inside the great room where we do all kinds of daily activities, including my work on this book.

The tree has become more than a simple physical tree in my love's yard. It also represents my new life with my love and even my love himself. Then there is the tree image that mystics use to show the *sefirot*, the divine attributes. With this tree as the theme of my art quilt, it becomes the archetype of not only trees and my love but an even larger picture of the Divine as it manifests in my life.

This is your opportunity to choose a personal object of your own divine imagery for this project. Take your time exploring your environment by taking a stroll outdoors or looking through some favorite books and magazines. There will be lots of choices, but one will step forward as the perfect candidate.

Supplies

 Camera

 Tracing paper, pencil, ruler, eraser

 Assortment of cotton quilting fabric

 Quilting thread and needles

 Embroidery thread and needles

 Embellishments as desired

Directions

1. Using your camera, decide on an object, place, or thing that will be the subject of your quilt. Take lots of photographs and pick the one or ones that will inspire your quilt.

2. Decide on the finished size of your quilt without borders. Create a grid on the tracing paper that gives you the full surface of the quilt. For example, for my quilt, which is 20 inches by 24 inches, I made a 5-by-6 grid, or 30 4-inch squares. Create a smaller grid of the same proportion on tracing paper for your photo.

3. Using your grid photo as a guide, make a full-size outline of your image in pencil on your larger tracing-paper grid.

4. Make a second tracing of the image over the top of the first. Use this to draw in background lines and then as the pattern to piece the background.

5. Select background fabrics and piece by hand or machine.

6. Select object fabrics. Number the tracing paper pieces, cut them apart, and use them to cut the fabrics. Add ¼-inch seam allowance to all edges when cutting.

7. Pin the fabric pieces onto the background. Appliqué the pieces by hand using an invisible slip stitch and turning under the ¼-inch seam.

8. Add borders as desired. Refer to chapter 1 for some border instructions.

9. If you wish to embellish your quilt top, this is the time. You can use such things as embroidery, ribbons, buttons, rubberstamps, or ink.

10. Make a quilt sandwich with the top, batting, and backing. Pin or baste together.

11. Quilt as desired, by hand or by machine. I used a thick metallic embroidery thread and large noticeable stitches. In hand quilting we hide the knots at the beginning and the end in the batting, as shown in the illustrations to the right.

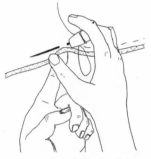

Hand quilting.

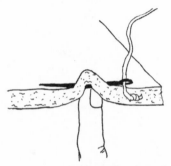

Beginning a thread.

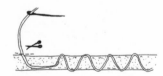

Ending a thread.

12. Trim the batting and the backing to match the top. Add the sleeve on the back for hanging (see introduction, p. 16) and finish the quilt with the binding.

Variations

- Remake the same pattern using a completely different color scheme.

- Make another quilt applying the same process to another of your photographs.

- Make the quilt a second time on a different scale, either much larger or much smaller.

- Make a folk art quilt of your current home.

- Make a folk art quilt of the home of your dreams.

FRAGMENTS OF LIFE
Remembrance Crazy Quilt

Netzach: *dominance, victory, eternity, conquest, the capacity to overcome.*

When my partner Heath died, we were in the midst of a struggle. My late beloved was an obsessive collector. Was he bitten by the bug because he was a vagabond, an itinerant actor, living most of his life without a home? Or maybe it had nothing to do with needing a place and was instead his purely cultivated tastes and larger-than-life loves. We'll never know for sure, but my bet is that it was a combination of both of these and more.

Heath spent his entire adult life moving about, setting up one temporary home after another. In each new place, he would rebuild his nest, buying whatever creature comforts he found necessary to maintain a quality life. At the close of each location, he chose to store the acquired possessions, planning to retrieve them at a future date.

Heath had many interests, stemming from his life as a Canadian-born professional actor. First and foremost was his adoration of the written and spoken word. He was a word master. He was a devotee of the British, both their culture and history. His Buddhist practice attracted him to Indian and Japanese culture. His avocation as a drum major in a Scottish pipe band accentuated his passion for music and uniforms with all of their pomp and circumstance. These affinities comprised only the surface layer.

Heath collected books, scripts, playbills, videos, audios, props, costumes, uniforms, hats, walking sticks, religious artifacts, and toy soldiers. Separate from the formal collections, he kept every contract, review, and photo related to his long and prestigious career. He also kept every artifact related to our eight-year relationship, but that's a whole different story. He titled his collections "an embarrassment of riches."

To give you a very small example, when sorting his videos I found nineteen different years of the Queen of England's birthday parade. That's right, nineteen unique videos on one very specific theme. Heath was consistently over the top. He did everything in full flower, acquiring each and every—and then some—object related to the various subjects that caught his interest.

In 1999, after two years of my following him around the world, we discovered that he had an incurable case of prostate cancer. To have regular treatment, he relinquished his vagabond life to stay with me in Pittsburgh. As we acknowledged the ending of his life, it became imperative to me that he dispose of all the items in storage, not leaving them in my reluctant hands. Getting Heath to face this reality wasn't a pretty picture. By the time he had unloaded, as he called it, his entire ego wagon from storage, our loft was overflowing with hundreds of carefully packaged and labeled boxes housing his multiple collections.

I have done quite a bit of sorting and purging, but it will take years to disperse his collections. The only thing I can be sure of is that his fibers will eventually make their way into quilts. The first of these was a Birds-in-Air T-shirt quilt made from Heath's beloved T-shirt collection. To accent the T-shirts, I included his special compilation of red dharma cloth pieces and a kid's twin bed blanket from his childhood. Because he and I had a mutual connection to birds, I picked the Birds-in-Air patchwork pattern. Everything contained within the quilt—every stitch and patch, the pattern and the backing—allow me to be in his presence even though he is no longer alive. He inadvertently collected the shirts for me rather than for himself, as I am the one using the quilt.

How does one deal with the loss of a loved one? Being a quilt maker, I always knew about the great tradition of remembrance quilts. A remembrance quilt is any quilt created to remember something of significance. It can be a person, an event, or a realization—any important life experience the quilt maker wants to immortalize in fabric. Creating these quilts opens a space to reflect, recall, weep, lament, sigh, smile, and laugh. There are lots of different kinds of remembrance quilts: friendship quilts that mark relationships, special occasion quilts that document events such as births and weddings, and mourning quilts that mark the loss of a loved one.

One example of a remembrance quilt is the monumental quilt fashioned by the loved ones of AIDS victims. The first time I actually saw a portion of the AIDS quilt was on a special trip to the New York Public Library. I saw panels that were rough and not professionally crafted, yet each was very powerful to me because I knew it represented a precious extinguished life. That was many years ago. Today, every conceivable material and technique has been used throughout the quilt: photographs, letters, and even personal items like rubber flip-flops and teddy bears have been lovingly incorporated. Too big to be contained in the Washington Monument Mall where it used to be shown periodically, sections now travel around the country. Don't miss the opportunity to go and see it. It is a powerful visual expression. Its blocks represent the precious individuality of the victims, and the quilt in its entirety represents the wretched nature of the disease. It is a powerful experience for all concerned: an artwork that speaks beyond words.

Well-versed quilters know about the most distinctive historical memory quilt to survive today. It is Elizabeth Roseberry Mitchell's Graveyard Quilt. It has a central medallion that is a fenced graveyard with four named coffins. The bulk of the quilt, surrounding the graveyard, is alternating star and solid block, with an outside fencelike border with a dozen or so more named coffins.

Elizabeth produced the quilt in the 1830s to help her grieve the loss of her son, John Vannatta. He was two years and eight months old when he died. At that time, a good housekeeper saved every fabric fragment, so that nothing was wasted. Patchwork was one example of this economy. For this quilt, she stitched together tiny remnants from the shirts and dresses of her children. Every bit was precious. The quilt became the only record of her son as there were no death records kept at that time in Ohio, where she was living.

After my parents died, I produced over twenty pieces using their clothing and textiles. I made embroideries, a linen jacket, a poncho, table runners, photo-transfer books, and a range of pieces big and small. I even transformed the scraps into usable squares and strips to make traditional patterned bed covers, one for each of the seven grandchildren.

I cleaned out my parents' belongings twice, once to move both of them to an assisted-living facility and the final time after my dad's death. Both times, along with photos and special mementos, I was overwhelmed with the array of memories I carted back to my studio. I specifically selected clothing and textiles that I hoped would be quilt worthy. There were numerous cross-stitched tablecloths, all kinds of knitted sweaters, fancy formal wear, brightly colored golf attire, and heavy Turkish towels. The fabric piles were unruly, requiring continual sorting, ripping, and discarding, and I had trouble throwing any of the precious cloth away.

The strongest memory I have of the actual quilting experience is the first time I cut and ripped off one of the pant legs from my dad's tux. Ripping that leg gave me a powerful, direct understanding of his death, the clear reality that I had no choice but to destroy these pants. He had no more use for them. It became my responsibility to make them over into something new. I was letting go of Dad and transforming the pants to a different and useful existence.

From the beginning of my mission, one photo had held my attention. It showed Mom and Dad as a young, carefree couple strutting on the boardwalk of Atlantic City. I translated the image to a life-size pattern and began to sort the fabrics. I was dismayed. My parents appeared light and airy in the photo, while the materials were overwhelmingly heavy and coarse. In frustration, I covered over the life-size drawing and began a quilt more in keeping with the materials. What resulted was a child's view of my parents, complete with our house, my brother, and my father's two brothers from whom he was inseparable. I spent uncountable days on this first quilt, cutting into the clothing, hacking off sleeves, salvaging pockets, and ripping linings. Every stitch was by hand, fueled by memories and tears. As I was adding decorative embroideries to the quilt's surface, I got that typical quilt maker's yen to create yet another piece that would be some variation of the first. Before I knew it, I had a series worthy of a show for our local community-center art museum.

The blowup sketch of my parents on the boardwalk remained untouched on my pinup board. Other projects came and went: commissions, exhibition work, and more memory pieces. In time the solution came to me. Instead of their clothing fabric, I went to the magnificent collection of silks they had purchased for me while on their travels. At my request, they had bought me several meters (39 inches) of both blue and red silk. I have held onto the fabric for years. It was too precious and at the same time too difficult to use. I needed a bigger purpose for these gems. Finally I had it.

Sadye and Howie is a silk appliqué quilt and the culmination of my memory-quilt grieving process. I had the quilt of my parents as I chose to remember them, light and airy, young and hopeful, and as my mom would have said, "full of piss and vinegar." It took me two years to cut up their clothing. It was the only way I knew to grieve my loss. In the process I created a memorial that would have filled them with pride along with tinges of embarrassment and disbelief.

As I was finishing the final preparations to mount my show Pieces of Memory at our local community center, I happened to meet an interior-designer friend. "What are you working on these days?" I asked her. "Funeral homes," she replied. My reaction was immediate, "That's funny. It could be that I have a product for funeral homes." That brief exchange launched the business of producing memory quilts for others.

Today, I make use of my experiences to make memory quilts from the memorial cloth of others. An older mother gave her son a wall hanging made of Boy Scout uniforms and badges to celebrate his thirtieth birthday. A mother and her four daughters commissioned five shawls made from the ties of the men of the family. I worked with a fifty-year-old and her friends in an all-day quilt-making birthday celebration. I've made prayer shawls out of T-shirts, baby quilts out of wedding dresses, and quilted clothing out of European embroidery. Silk ties have combined with woolen suits, formal wear has united with hand-knit sweaters, and sports caps have merged with baby blankets, to name a precious few.

Netzach of Past, Present, and Future

Netzach is most often translated as victory or conquest. We might also use words such as security, revelation, eternity, or even determination. *Netzach* has the power to conquer, and in that way it risks overwhelming. When it is in balance with the other divine attributes of the *sefirot*, it actively overcomes limitations and obstacles and creates the way for order and the resulting victory.

Netzach is essential for self-expression and actualization. It is relating to the core of our beings, the place from which we recognize our own sense of power in the world. All these descriptions allude to our primary purpose. Through *netzach*, we become aware and are able to actualize the divine plan that is available for each and every one of us.

We find *netzach* at the lower right side of the Tree of Life, which is the part that acts directly with our actual world of experience. It balances with *hod* from the lower left side of the tree to help us maintain our sense of self and at the same time surrendering to it in a balance of giving and taking. Accompanying it is the profound urge to accomplish something and to be assertive.

The right side of the tree is in line with the more expansive qualities of *chesed* and *chochmah*. Being on the expansive side, *netzach* has the power to overwhelm and take on more importance than is sometimes healthy.

Moses is the archetype of *netzach*. He was a master of leadership. He created the platform on which a nation could take shape. He was one of the few humans to receive direct transmission from the Divine. Providence was imposed upon him without choice in many forms at many times. The *netzach* experience is completely beyond our ability to reason, and in that way it can overwhelm the senses and our personal identity. The Divine imposes its will and prevails against any obstacle that might block divine giving and receiving. When operating simultaneously in all ten directions and five dimensions—north, south, east, west, up, down, time, space, good, and evil—we become pure being. This is the ultimate potential of the mind and the level at which the divine spark of the soul interacts with the infinite in absolute unity. The mind of a prophet, someone of the caliber of Moses, operates at this level. Prophecy can bring together the past, present, and future.

Faith becomes trust as it lives. Trust is active faith. Trust is associated with the inner infinite attribute of *netzach*. Trusting the Divine translates to trusting life by living totally in the present and letting go of past and future. This becomes the expression of a person's inner understandings and security, which ultimately depends upon our faith in the meaning and immortality of life. By living in the present, everything forces us deeper and deeper into the reality of life with awareness and trust in divine providence.

Letting Go

Grieving is about letting go. It is integrating loss into our lives, making a large enough container to actually hold and cherish the grief. There is no other choice. Grief softens our hearts so we can expand and integrate the life changes and allow loss its right to full participation. With this integration, we have access to our grief as we need it, and we use it as another life-learning tool.

Heath, my mom, my dad, and all the others I have lost are still a part of me, just in a form different from the physical. I call upon them daily through a reminiscent sound, color, story, place, thought, thing, and, of course, cloth. Our goal becomes living the losses of life as a celebration of life, a gratitude for what we have and being with what is. This kind of choiceless living is actually quite a relief.

We can apply this idea of grieving to our daily lives. Loss occurs countless times a day in every conceivable situation. We expect something to happen one way, and inevitably the result is not what we wanted or expected. What does letting go mean? It means that we understand that there is no separation between ourselves and the circumstances of our life. Whatever the circumstances are, this is our life. With that kind of open-hearted acceptance, we become free enough to get into the work and do whatever needs to be done.

Heath had a great answer when friends would ask about his health. The first and only words out of his mouth would be, "I have no complaints whatsoever. Everything is just as it is supposed to be."

The way to true *netzach* victory is through acceptance and nonattachment. Our spiritual practice can achieve a more sophisticated level of action by accepting and letting go at the same time.

In Zen practice we say, "Experience the body and breath." When following the breath, we do not control it. Control is dualistic because we are exerting our will on something as though it were a separate thing. Instead, with an integrated view, we experience the breath being with what is. That is the solution to life's problems: to experience the difficulty of what's going on, be with it, and then to act compassionately based on the truth, or reality, of experience. We often expend our energies avoiding and complaining, being the victim, and trying to maintain control.

This quilting project is a direct opportunity to transform the unhelpful need to control into being with and accepting what is. Begin by choosing some material with deep-seated memory and meaning—something that is very precious to you. By giving it up, letting it go, and transforming it, you will have the true heart of victory.

Crazy Quilting

In this chapter we will make a Crazy Quilt where fabrics are attached to a muslin foundation and decorated with hand embroidery stitches. Crazy Quilts are characterized by a miscellaneous potpourri of fabrics cut into irregular patches of random size and shape with no central theme, no planned single design, and no uniformity. The distinctive feature of this quilt is the irregularity itself. Elaborate embroidery stitches and embellishments show up on nearly every seam and patch, and often there are further attachments such as buttons, jewelry, and appliqué.

The Industrial Revolution, which occurred in the last two decades of the nineteenth century during Queen Victoria's reign, made segments of American society rich. These nouveau-riche families had much leisure time on their hands, as they could afford servants to do the mundane work. Crazy Quilts became popular as a pastime when women's lives were governed by strict codes of behavior. For a genteel lady, needlework was considered a proper use of her leisure time. Victorian gentlewomen used fancy fabrics because they could afford these beautiful treasures. What better use of this leisure time than to sew bits of silk, velvet, and satin into a coverlet and embroider upon the seams?

The name *Victoria* comes from the Latin word meaning "victory," which is also the meaning of *netzach*. The Crazy Quilt craze was an abrupt departure from traditional patch work and appliqué designs. The period as a whole was characterized by rigid standards and overdecoration, which pervaded every aspect of life from architecture and music to social customs. This new quilting style provided women with

137

a meaningful, limited opportunity to break out of societal constraints and create quilts without a prescribed set of standards as to content, design, and fabric use. To emphasize this opportunity, Crazy Quilts were made in sizes too small for beds and migrated from their traditional place in the bedroom to become works of art displayed in the parlor. The Crazy Quilt story illustrates the triumph of women's imaginativeness and ingenuity in the face of limiting trials and tribulations—a kind of letting go.

The Crazy Quilt is not quilted like a typical quilt. There are neither quilting stitches nor battings employed in its construction. The finished product has just two layers and no batting. Without batting, it lies smoothly on a table, and objects can sit safely on it. Crazy Quilts arose in a time of material abundance when people were inclined to collect objects of all kinds. They functioned as complex textile scrapbooks. A single quilt often displayed a variety of fabrics, patterns, stitches, colors, textures, and embroidered images; and such items as tobacco premiums, fair ribbons, signatures, or dress and tie scraps of important people would appear in the quilt. Like all collections, they became highly idiosyncratic and specialized.

The practice of randomly piecing odd bits of cloth together was a money-saving habit gleaned from earlier times. In the harsh and unfamiliar environment of the new world, the early settlers had to work hard and be responsible, first to the family and then to the community, to build a strong and enduring society. When the coverlets and blankets that the colonists had brought with them began to wear out, they were first patched, until the cloth could no longer hold thread, and then they were recycled. Worn parts were cut away, and any useful pieces were recombined. From these pieced odds and ends, the Crazy Quilt came into being. Red plaid woolen underwear might be sewn next to a triangle of silk cut from a nightgown. Beside a remnant of chintz sofa, we might find the cotton from a summer dress. In later Victorian times, the quilts included scraps of silk, velvet, brocade, plush satin, wool, cotton, and linen. Bits of a wedding dress might be sewn next to a remnant from a scarlet uniform. These combinations resulted more by accident than by design.

Crazy Quilts were for the most part made in blocks, the square units of design that make up a quilt. The designer determined the size of the quilt and then decided just how many blocks she wished to put into it. She would begin with background blocks of coarsely woven sack cloth and proceed by attaching irregular pieces from her collection.

Crazy patchwork reached its peak in the late 1880s, with the most elaborate work so ornamented with intricate embroidery that the fabric itself was hardly visible. The technique continued in popularity until around 1920. After that, there would always be a few quilt makers drawn to the technique for its unique use of odds and ends. This quilting technique works in support of our letting-go efforts.

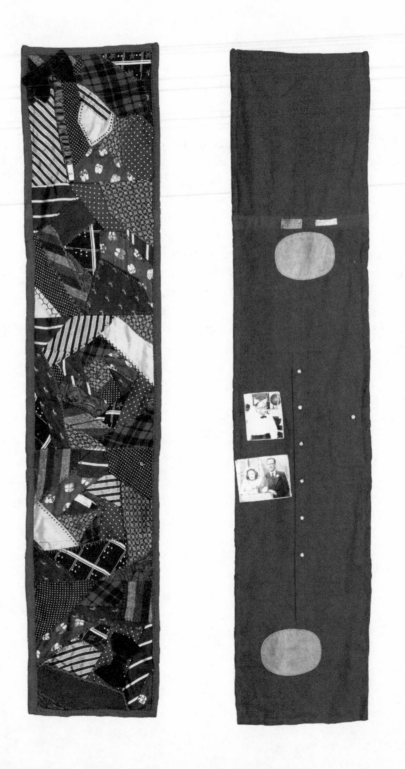

CRAZY QUILT TABLE RUNNER

Each of us has a bag of memories associated with our clothing and textiles. Life's constant change leaves tangible tactile surfaces as a handy reminder. Our project is a table runner that will be 12 inches wide and multiples of 12 inches in length. You can put as many squares as necessary in a line to fit the length of your table.

Supplies

> 1 yard muslin (or the amount necessary for the size of your project)
>
> 1 yard backing (or the amount necessary for the size of your project)
>
> An assortment of cloth that holds special meaning for you
>
> Quilting thread
>
> Cotton embroidery floss in assorted colors
>
> Optional: Photo transfers

Directions

1. For these blocks we are using ½-inch seam allowances around the outside edges. To end up with a 12-inch square, cut a 13-inch square of muslin. Cut as many of these squares as you need. For example, if you want a table runner that finishes at 12 inches by 60 inches, cut 5 blocks of muslin.

2. Select your favorite fabric from your grouping and roughly cut out a 2- to 3-inch square. Don't worry if the angles are not exactly square. In this case, the finished product will actually be more interesting if the patches are oddly sized. Lay this piece at the approximate center of one of the muslin blocks. You don't have to be exact about this either as the block will end up being asymmetrical anyway.

3. Select a second fabric that contrasts in texture or color with the first. Cut a random-size piece, making

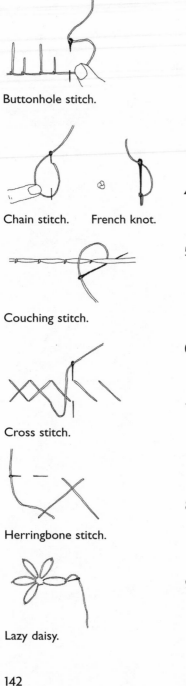

Buttonhole stitch.

Chain stitch.   French knot.

Couching stitch.

Cross stitch.

Herringbone stitch.

Lazy daisy.

sure that one edge is as long as one of the edges of the first patch. Lay these two fabrics with right sides facing each other, matching up that one similar length edge. This second fabric will be covering both the first fabric and the muslin block underneath it. Use quilting thread to hand stitch a running stitch ¼ inch from that matching edge. This is one of those circumstances where it's easier and more fun to work by hand, but if you prefer the machine, that will work equally well.

4. Turn the second piece to show its right side. The sewn edge is now hidden, and you now have two fabric pieces sewn to each other and the muslin.

5. Continue in this fashion, adding different random-sized fabric pieces and working your way out from the center until the muslin is completely covered. Trim any excess that goes beyond the muslin edge, ending up with a 13-inch square.

6. Complete all the blocks in this fashion and piece them into one long row. You have completed the crazy quilt top.

7. Now you can add decorative embroidery stitches over the top of as many of the seams as you like. The more embroidery you do, the better it will look. Start with a simple backstitch and feel free to experiment with a variety of stitches and thread colors.

8. When all the embroidery is completed, cut a backing fabric that is 1 inch bigger along all four edges of the Crazy Quilt top. Lay the patchwork top on top of the backing, wrong sides facing each other.

9. Fold the outside edges of the backing in to meet the outside edge of the top, and then fold the backing in once again to form a binding around the outside edge of the Crazy Quilt top. Hand stitch the binding in place, and add embroidery to the bound edge as you desire.

Variations

- Photo-transfer and appliqué meaningful photos to your Crazy Quilt.

- Expand the number of blocks to make a Crazy Quilt throw.

- Make two larger Crazy Quilt blocks to use as the outside of a carry-all bag.

- Make a Crazy Quilt kimono jacket. Cut the pattern pieces out of muslin, and then use the shaped pieces of muslin instead of squares to apply the crazy quilt pieces.

- Make blocks using the Log Cabin pattern with Crazy Quilting embroidery for a little more control of color and design.

- Research and practice more complex embroidery stitches for future projects.

COLLECTING
SOUVENIRS

T-shirt Quilt

Yesod: *foundation; the longing to connect.*

Friends had come to spend the night with me. They were on their way for a little escape to see the Frank Lloyd Wright houses about an hour southwest of Pittsburgh. It was such a fun visit. This mother-daughter team came in the late afternoon and took a tour of my loft, and we walked to dinner at my favorite Japanese restaurant. Then my daughter joined us for a game of dominos accompanied with Rocky Road ice cream, Back to Nature peanut butter cookies, and Earl Grey tea. We had a wonderful evening. I felt like I was at the beach. That's how I know these friends, from my yearly summer jaunts to the Jersey shore.

Various family members and friends have gathered at Long Beach Island in New Jersey since the 1980s. The way I feel about owning quilts applies equally to this situation: the more the merrier. The main organizer is one of my contemporaries and a long-time friend. Our original connection was through a quilting class I taught at a mother's-day-out program when our children were young. Mother's day out is a great way for stay-at-home parents and their kids to have a social experience.

Our beach organizer is a prime example of the many wonderful friends I've made through teaching. In this case, we were both young mothers who saw the importance of full-time child raising yet wanted and needed support to pursue our personal adult interests. That quilting stage translated to projects such as patchwork children's clothing and tot-size bed quilts.

Our family connection continues to this day at our summer hangout, a typical family-style beach town, including little

houses with outdoor showers and gas grills, a clear unclut-
tered beach dotted with the newest in ocean paraphernalia,
and a main street with lots of seafood restaurants, big
breakfasts, ice cream, miniature golf, and souvenir T-shirt
shops. The people who gather there are a mix of ages and
life situations, blending together through the common draw
of the ocean.

The beach day has a simple routine, with early morning
walks by the bay and afternoon walks along the shore,
leisurely reading, stitching, or snoozing, then late afternoon
beach conversations, hot showers, simple grilled meals. By
evening, everyone gathers together for silly games of cha-
rades and the like. It's a luxury connecting with loving people in this relaxed setting of uncomplicated joy. People who
normally see little of each other find themselves sharing good
talks and making deep connections.

Any vacation is an opportunity for me to do some fiber
form purely for my personal pleasure. If it is quilting, it's
likely to be miniature, something easy to carry around yet
full of challenge and detail. Another possibility is my favorite
stitching activity: pictures made entirely of French knot
embroidery. In general, I try never to go anywhere without a
knitting or crocheting project within arm's reach. One summer, I brought portable machines and we made carry-all bags
similar to those in chapter 5. Next summer, I'm considering
embroidery expressing mystical concepts, something that I
want to do but can't seem to squeeze into my regular home-
stitching life. I locate a small corner of the beach house with
good light, set up a makeshift studio, and go back and forth
to the work as I desire. Part of the vacation joy is being able
to include some separate and special fiber project.

Pittsburgh has three rivers, but they lack the expansive
nature of the ocean—its sounds and its textures. The larger-
than-life regularity and repetitious change of the ocean provides serenity, solitude, and a peaceful contentment,
harboring a space for contemplation and discovery.

Returning to the ocean year after year is symbolic of the ebb and flow of life. The repetitious, yet ever-changing ocean waves express the necessity of change with their repeated withdrawal and encroachment onto the beach. One of my favorite traditional quilt patterns is called Ocean Waves. Little triangles surrounding a solid square give the eye both the active movement of the waves and the solid stability of the beach. Each plays its part in the flow and the cycle.

The ocean experience with my beach buddies allows me to relax and play as part of a group. Over the years, I've participated in a multitude of groups with a variety of purposes: quilting, artistic, political, neighborhood, exercise, reading, social, and spiritual. At one point I had so many group affiliations that I wondered if it wasn't some kind of addictive behavior. To analyze my attraction, I found the ultimate group: a group that analyzes groups. I enrolled in Gestalt professional training.

In German, the word *gestalt* means shape. A gestalt is a structure or pattern of psychological phenomena that is integrated and constitutes a functional unit. The whole relationship is more than the sum of its parts; it is its own form. In Gestalt theory our behavior is not a series of individual elements, but an intrinsic nature of the whole. Gestalt therapy works by determining the nature of such wholes.

Gestalt training helped me analyze how I am in groups. I wasn't surprised to discover that I used group situations as an opportunity to hide. It is easy to blend within a group and avoid taking any risks by standing out as separate. In each interaction, each gestalt, there is a beginning, a middle, and an end. Not wanting to expose myself to the group, I had little tricks to avoid direct contact. I would always arrive late and leave early, in an effort to avoid beginnings and endings. I survived the middle phase by being quiet and reserved while in the group. The professional training provided an opportunity for me to pinpoint and understand my weaknesses and practice techniques to encourage full participation in all aspects of group situations. I could then join a group with the intention of actively benefiting and being useful and leave behind my tendency to hide.

Yesod, Our Longing to Connect

Yesod, or foundation, represents our perfect reciprocal relationship on the Tree of Life. It parallels the sixth day of creation when the animal kingdom including humans came into being. We are instructed to be fruitful and multiply, to grow and expand in divine benevolent consciousness. We are given the additional obligation to rule over the animals, the birds, and the fish, meaning that we can transcend our limited animal nature and fulfill a higher divine plan. Our drive to participate comes through *yesod.*

Tiferet harmonizes and balances *chesed* and *gevurah* to form a stable triangle. *Yesod* harmonizes and balances *netzach* and *hod* in a similar threesome. In addition, *yesod* has the unique aspect of being the channel to *malkhut,* our physical world. As a channel of communication, it is the conduit of spirit, making sure that light and life force reach their proper destination. This gives *yesod* an additional name, *emet,* truth.

Yesod and *malkhut* are part of an internal bond of love and understanding between giver and receiver. *Yesod* arouses the desire to receive in *malkhut. Malkhut* arouses the desire to give in *yesod. Yesod* joins creation in a bond of empathy and love to draw compassion and goodness into the world.

Yesod is the channel to the outside world for our mind and emotions. It controls the nature and strength of all our communication, allowing us to deepen our feelings and compassion for others. When we feel a close bond, a full sense of communication with another person, it is because we have formed a *yesod* bond. A strong *yesod* connection strengthens our own feelings of adequacy and wholeness.

Yesod, in the triangle with *netzach* and *hod,* balances aloneness and togetherness within relationships. *Yesod* is the channel through which *tiferet* strives to unite with the *Shekhinah* and pass on the creative and benevolent divine forces. *Yesod* is the power to contact, connect, and communicate with outer reality. With *yesod*'s ability to connect, it also exemplifies our sexual nature and reproductive functions. *Yesod* is the body's physical manifestation to authenticate and fulfill itself.

One of the most beautifully sensuous love poems from Western literature appears in the Hebrew Bible between Ecclesiastes and Isaiah. The Song of Solomon, also called the Song of Songs, uses powerfully seductive images to tell us of the passionate longing of young lovers who meet and separate and then describe one another's beauty. On the simple level, it is a love poem with many shifts of person, mood, and scene. The setting is ancient Palestine with rich use of striking natural images such as grapes, pomegranates, gazelles, and flowers.

In first-century Palestine, the Song of Songs was sung in taverns. In the Middle Ages, the text held a deep fascination for monks and nuns who would often transcribe the words. Mystics use its language to express their longing for oneness with the universe. Today, its lines are regularly incorporated into wedding ceremonies. I almost always use both Hebrew and English quotes from this poetry when I make a wedding quilt. The text is rich in its exploration of erotic love's relation between the physical and the spiritual. It strives to encourage us to use physical love as a transcendental experience to a higher expression of love.

So much of our modern lives maintain patterns of differentiation. Science separates the physical from the spiritual. Contemporary media separates love from sexuality. We yearn for a compassionate expression of our love. Our longing propels us to find a source of spirituality that treats us as whole human beings in which emotion, passion, and reason are all parts of a whole. The Song of Songs expresses this longing, which permeates the encounter of body and soul. It unites erotic tension with spiritual love in an intense and passionate allegory of our loving relationships with all. It exemplifies the intensity available beyond simple pleasure, where giving and receiving are one act, and our entire being is absorbed in this reciprocal relationship.

Reaching Out to Others with Affirmations

There was a telephone commercial awhile back with the line "Reach out and touch someone." Quilt makers are drawn to the tactile nature of things. Touch is our umbilical cord; it puts us squarely into a three-dimensional tactile world of patting, pinching, picking, pulling, scratching, tickling, holding, stroking, caressing, hugging, and kissing. There are many metaphors of touch in the language. When we care deeply about something, we say that we are touched. When we have a problem, we may say that it is thorny or sticky, or we may talk about someone or something that needs to be handled with kid gloves. Just as threads connect fabric, our hands connect us to others. Hands convey emotion. We pride ourselves that our products carry the label of being handmade.

A recurring notion in spiritual work is that nothing happens in isolation; everything is related. Yet quilting is easiest when we are alone. In many ways, quilting encourages isolation. We get a bit possessive of our ideas, techniques, and materials and find ourselves preferring to stay in our little nests. Quilters have a bumper sticker that reads: "The one who dies with the most fabric wins." The slogan pokes fun at our desire to hoard and hold onto more and more even though experience tells us there's no point. We can't take it with us.

One thing that keeps us from letting go is our continuing need for perfection. There is a practice in some cultures of deliberately including a mistake in the work to acknowledge imperfection. My experience is that we don't have to plan for a mistake—mistakes happen in the natural course of creation. We are perfectly imperfect humans. We will make mistakes, and instead of bemoaning the fact that we're not perfect, let's use the information gleaned from the mistake as an opportunity for learning and growth.

Along with possessiveness, jealousy, the most dangerous of all emotions, limits our ability to make contact, to connect. Jealousy implies that there are limited amounts and does not take into account the abundance of the universe. Jealousy deprives us of our will to act, the key to our creativity. Jealousy is not simply envy. Envy is wistful while jealousy is angry and destructive. We tend to think of jealousy as a single emotion, but it is a bundle of feelings. Jealousy can manifest as anger, fear, hurt, betrayal, anxiety, agitation, sadness, paranoia, depression, loneliness, envy, covetousness, powerlessness, inadequacy, and exclusion. Jealousy is about fear. It is the insecurity within us that creates fear in our relationships. We see someone's quilt using the same fabrics as our own, and immediately we convince ourselves that the other one is better than ours. When we are jealous, we fear losing something highly valued, and with that fear, we feel hurt, anger, and shame.

Jealousy is about fear of the unknown, fear of change, fear of losing power or control in a relationship, fear of scarcity and loss, and fear of abandonment. It is a reflection of our own insecurity about our worthiness, anxiety about being adequate as an artist. It brings forth all our doubts about our projects. For every jealous feeling, there is an emotion behind the jealousy, such as an unmet need, or a deep fear that our needs will not be met. This source of the jealousy is more significant than the jealousy itself. Recognizing those fears and unmet needs is the key to unmasking jealousy and taking away its power. Jealousy is just the finger pointing at the fears and needs we are afraid to face. When jealousy kicks in, it is the ancient reptilian part of our brain going into a fight or flight response because we feel that our very survival is threatened. When you feel jealous, ask yourself, "What is it that I am really afraid of? What do I need to make this situation safe for me? What is the worst thing that could happen and how likely is that to happen?"

Fulfillment, peace, joy, and abundance are available to us when we consciously embrace these ideas, constructively directing our thoughts through affirmations. If we sit in silence and think of another, we can sense in the other the same longing to be heard, to be noticed, to communicate, to be accepted and belong, to be understood, and to be with divinity. If we look inside each person, we can see his or her common humanity, as well as the individual spirit. Each of us carries the same loving concern for our quilting. Each has his or her own form of suffering. Let's not allow our false beliefs to separate us from one another. Understand and accept that each of us is doing his or her very best in any given situation.

Regardless of our state of mind, beliefs, or the language we speak, we all long to belong to the divine plan. We all want to return home to our place in the garden. Yet how often do fear and shame drive us out of the garden? How often does rejection by our peers threaten our existence in the garden? How often do our differences disconnect us from one another? But the Divine comes to us and invites us home to share in the feast of life. The Divine sees the depths of our hearts and our yearning to belong. The longing within each of us is why we will put the effort into our quilt making. It is our answer to our longing to connect; it is our path home. Sometimes we attempt to connect to external things such as possessions and power in an effort to connect to our deepest longing. So when we are in our nests quilting away, we shouldn't be surprised at who is right there with us. We don't look at externals but instead look within our hearts and see clearly all that is available for us.

Try saying this affirmation aloud: "My life is whole and complete. I am where I am meant to be at this moment in my life. I feel the light, energy, and wisdom that are an inherent part of who I am. I am a product of the creative spirit and I am a spirit who creates. I accept that my life has an ebb and flow of change, and I can make a positive effort to adjust as needed. I am filled with harmony and balance. The more love and compassion I give out to others, the more I shall receive in return."

Quilting Connections

Imagine living before the Industrial Revolution when families were large and women and men worked all day long as manual laborers. Every home had family members who sewed and mended clothing and bed covers. Much of what we buy today without a thought had to be produced at home in the past. Social time with family and neighbors was a limited refreshing highlight, and what could be better than combining work with the fun of gathering together to quilt?

The old-fashioned quilting bee was a social activity with a mission. The person who had completed the quilt top would organize the event. On the day of the quilting bee, the quilters would arrive early and begin marking the quilt top with quilting patterns. In those days, they marked with chalk, or the more costly cinnamon, and used plates, thimbles, and tea cups to trace the quilting patterns—or anything to mark the placement of their fine hand-quilted stitches. The layers were basted onto a long wooden quilting frame that would allow several stitchers to work at one time.

Stitching would commence and continue on through the day, as the quilters attempted to finish the work before the nonquilters showed up in the late afternoon for dinner and country dancing with fiddles. The quilting bee was an important social event.

Even in those days, quilts took on more roles than mere providers of warmth. There were quilts to make political statements, to raise funds, to acknowledge important friendships, and to honor life events. That tradition continues today, with quilting projects exploring the environment, politics, tragedies, and health issues. Quilts with messages of hope and healing for the earth become a metaphor for comforting the victims and mending the world. Quilts offer love, security, warmth, and comfort, raising the awareness of everyone's need to heal. Quilting provides fun and rewarding service opportunities for individuals and groups.

Today there are all kinds of quilting groups in every community that foster and perpetuate a love of quilting. The activities are a great source of inspiration and encouragement. Guilds exist to exchange information and ideas, educate their members, and provide a place for people to enjoy the fellowship of other quilters. Everyone is welcome—novices and recognized experts, young and old, men and women. Activities include lectures, workshops, challenge quilts, and special projects. Locate these groups on the Internet, by word of mouth, from articles in the newspaper, from local quilt shops, as part of church groups—or start your own.

You will find lots of ways to get out into the community with your quilting. Look to your conflicts as one possible opportunity. Find or create a quilting group that can engage in public conversation and help seek common ground and consensus. As you look for compatriots, go beyond your stereotypes and prejudices. Use the quilting to empower the powerless, to support peace efforts, and to teach the children. Spread service, thanks, laughter, and joy through the natural connection of quilting.

T-SHIRT QUILT

My brother lives in a beach community in Florida, where my family has congregated over many winter vacations. Our regular morning activity was a walk on the boardwalk followed by a yummy breakfast at one of the many hotels along the ocean. It was the reward of food that got us going on the walk.

My best source of entertainment on the walk was to read the slogans on T-shirts worn by people walking in the opposite direction. The sayings and slogans said a lot about the people—where they were from, where they had been, their group identification, their politics, and their relationships to others.

Each of us has at least one drawer full of T-shirts. Each shirt represents a vacation, event, or statement. They are all sizes, shapes, and colors. Some we never wear, while others become favorites, worn often. The T-shirt quilt turns those treasured logo images into a cohesive look as a quilt product.

Supplies

12–24 T-shirts with meaningful logo images

Fleece backing fabric

Sewing thread that matches fleece

Directions

1. Use your rotary cutter to cut out the logo images. We want each logo to have a layer of plain T-shirt under it. This double layer prevents the knit from stretching when sewing. Lay out the shirt with the logo design facing you. When the shirt is flat, place your 2-inch-wide see-through ruler at each edge of the design and cut along the outside edge of the ruler. Cut through the front and the back of the shirt at the same time, and then just throw away the excess.

2. Because each logo has a different dimension, the patches must be organized to fit into a rectangle.

Begin to group them in like sizes by width, and line them up into vertical rows. There are several ways to get the widths to match. You can subtract some of the extra 2-inch area remaining around the logo, or you can add borders of extra T-shirt material to either or both sides, or you can lay two smaller logos side by side to match the width of a bigger one. Also, consider a balance of color and design as you decide on the arrangement.

3. Once you have established the rows, you will begin the construction by sewing the shirt pieces into vertical columns. Again, in order to make all the verticals identical in length, you can subtract some of the 2-inch extra allowance or add some borders or an additional T-shirt piece.

4. Use the quilt-as-you-go method to sew the rows together (see Introduction, p. 15), and attach them to the fleece backing. Piece the fleece as necessary so that it is at least 3 inches larger than the finished quilt.

5. Lay out the fleece wrong side up. You will be constructing in straight vertical rows. Starting 3 inches from one edge, lay the first vertical row of logos right sides up and centered between the top-to-bottom edges of the fleece. Right sides together, pin the second row, matching top and bottom edges. Sew together at the seam allowance, at the same time sewing through the fleece.

6. Press the row flat carefully with a warm iron. You have to be careful that the iron doesn't touch any of the logos. Depending on the material, the heat may melt them. Check to be sure that all the seams are included and that the back is smooth. If you must make corrections, do it now. Once the next row is sewn on, you cannot go back.

7. Continue in this manner until all the vertical rows are attached.

8. Trim the fleece to 1½ inches larger than the T-shirt edges. Turn in the fleece twice to cover the edges. Stitch through all the layers.

Variations

- Take your quilt with you on your next vacation and have everyone sign it with permanent ink markers.

- Make a quilt for your favorite sports enthusiast, with all their special team numbers and logos.

- Instead of a quilt, try a soft quilt book format. Create 8-inch by 10-inch fabric pages, place them back to back, and bind them together at one edge.

- Make another T-shirt Quilt, adding related photo transfers.

- Instead of fleece, use an old sheet or blanket of significance and batting.

TIES THAT BIND
Rail Fence Signature Tablecloth

Malkhut: *kingdom; the physical world, solidity and stability, pure existence; the lowest level of creation furthest removed from the Divine source but also the level of greatest density, where the scheme of the Divine intent reaches its greatest elaboration.*

Recently I was the artist-in-residence for a spiritual community of women from eastern Pennsylvania. We met and spent the weekend together at a fabulous retreat center in Maryland. They wanted to have a fun bonding experience, like the camp days of their youth. I taught them about quilt making as an expression of spirituality through a group experience. We cut up their obsolete clothing and textiles and transformed them into a tablecloth for the group to use. It was an inspirational weekend for all of us.

My spiritual community is my meditation group. We meet in our homes twice each week in numbers varying from two to eighteen. The group itself is eleven years old. We were pulled together by the spiritual longing for a more direct connection to divinity.

We are women and men of varying ages and religions. We began by meeting Saturday afternoons for an hour every six weeks. We quickly moved to once a month and then every other week and finally to weekly. Sometime into the third year, we added a second meeting on Wednesday mornings. Presently, we meet on Saturday afternoons for two hours and on Wednesday mornings for an hour.

The agenda has been as variable as the meeting times. We started reading a text on Jewish meditation and then experimented with the ideas as we read them. We did meditation on candles and Hebrew letters. We did text study and audio instruction tapes, all in an exploratory effort to find a meditation system and a format for the group.

We also meet at least twice yearly for silent meditation retreats. Sometimes we have guest teachers. In addition, we encourage each other to explore specific individual interests and teachers. Sometimes it's only one of us, and at other times we go in a caravan to a workshop or a lecture.

The group encourages my visual and tactile interests. I have taught several of the members to quilt, knit, or crochet. One time we even took a field trip to our local yarn shop so that everyone could get help picking a new project. I have been able to make use of my true nature with visual meditations, and when the group sits at my house, everyone wraps him- or herself in a quilt.

There were a couple of funny little jokes I had about the group. Someone would ask me who was in the group, and I would name one of the members. That person would invariably ask something about the member, and then I would take great pleasure in saying, "I don't know. I only meditate with her."

The other funny thing is our decision-making process. We have never had a leader. We've had participants attempt it, only to be thwarted by what I lovingly call "the lowest common denominator." Nothing happens in our group without consensus. If we can't arrive at agreement on whatever it may be, it just doesn't happen.

We have one requirement for joining the group. Potential members must purchase and read *The Conscious Community*. It is a group manual written by a rabbi who lived in the Warsaw Ghetto in Poland at the start of World War II. He led a meditation group in the ghetto. The book holds a powerful truth about the nature and the requirements of being committed to a spiritual community. We have found that people either identify with the book and are drawn to our group, or they aren't. Requiring the text makes the group self-selecting.

About four years into the group, the weekday morning contingent decided to stay later every so often to talk and get to know one another a little bit. Finding more than meditation as common ground, we went on to have holiday celebrations, social nights of movies and dinner, and generally became each other's support systems for all of life's events. What appeared slow and haphazard, working to the lowest common denominator, has served us well. These are the people that I trust to be with me no matter what happens in my life.

One of the keys to the success of our group is that we don't have to follow the same meditation practice. We'll help newcomers with choices and techniques, but we each do our own thing. We share a lot of our explorations, and we use texts as the springboard to our learning. The main thing about our meditation is that it is experiential. We learn through doing. Things and ideas are revealed, practices present themselves, and we encourage and support each other in the pursuit of our longing to know the Divine within every molecule of our beings.

Malkhut, the Earth as Our Kingdom

Malkhut, kingdom, is the focal point of all of the divine attributes of the Tree of Life as they reach their final destination—us. It is both the beginning and the ending. As the receiver of all that has come before, it is the last step in the creation process, the materialization of the universe as we know it today. It is also the first step in our return to the Garden of Eden and oneness. As the receiver of all, the attributes are drawn into the earth, which contains everything.

The essence of *malkhut* is sovereignty and nobility, including reverence for life, faith in the absolute, and hope for the future. The essence is experiencing our quilting and ourselves as sanctuaries where divinity can reside. All the thoughts and emotions that flow through both our conscious and our unconscious are firmly rooted in our physical makeup. This is how we are perceived and how we perceive others.

Malkhut as the seventh day of creation is also considered the Sabbath, the day of rest. A day of contemplation, not doing and simply being, gives us time and space to appreciate the Divine's sustenance in the world and our lives.

Balance is a primary concept in Kabbalah as we look at the dualities throughout the *sefirot*. Here everything comes together, balancing the physical, emotional, psychological, and spiritual into a perfectly imperfect us. When we're balanced, we are in flow, and everything runs smoothly; we tap into our creativity with ease. The goal is to get to know ourselves so well that we create what we want rather than reacting emotionally to what comes to us. It means knowing our bodies, clearing our minds, opening our hearts, having direction, and taking action. As we search for a glimpse of our true selves, we allow for the mercy that understands that we are perfectly imperfect.

Rituals

A traditional cleansing practice in the Jewish tradition is the mikvah, a ritual bath. A mikvah is a natural body of pure running water. Today, most Jewish populations still operate one that serves the entire local community. The pool is designed specifically for immersion according to very specific rules and customs. Going to the mikvah means going from impure to pure, or renewal, through immersion in water.

Water is the primary source of all living things. It has the power to purify, to restore and replenish life. There are many ways to employ the mikvah. Women use it after menstruation. The mikvah immersion marks the end of a period of sexual abstinence between husband and wife, and thereby becomes part of a regular cycle in married life. From the onset of menstruation until mikvah immersion, couples refrain from marital relations. During this time, the marital couple expresses their husband-wife relationship without physical intimacy. The reunion that follows the immersion holds the highest potential for sanctity in marriage. Mikvah helps create a husband-wife relationship that is in a state of continuous renewal.

Mikvah immersion signals the final stage of conversion to Judaism. Religious men customarily use it at auspicious times, such as holidays or for a groom on his wedding day. Highly observant families will immerse new dishes in the mikvah before first-time use.

Rituals give a concrete shape to abstract spiritual ideals while adding color and zest to life. A wisely planned and solemnly conducted ritual prepares the ground, creates the atmosphere, suggests the mood, and predisposes the mind so that our spirits open to the mystery and wonder of the greater power.

Rituals mark a point in time. They evoke emotion, images, and memory. Each of us has a variety of family traditions and celebrations. There is always a theme for a ritual, a reason we come together. Often it is a life-cycle event, such as birth, coming of age, marriage, or death. Each ritual has unique components: special participants, favorite foods, special clothing and music, and a particular location. The event may have particular decorations or symbols associated with it. People may pray or share an oral history or folktale during it.

We all observe rituals. There are the standard social ones of our particular religion or society. There are other rituals and rites of passage, such as graduation from college or annual reunions with family, friends, and peers. Then there are those odd little rituals we do for ourselves—the special way we lay our fabrics when we work, or a particular beverage we have every morning. We often don't even realize we are doing something as a ritual because it seems so commonplace and natural to us.

There are rituals that others employ that might appear pagan and uncivilized, from some other time and culture that we don't understand. One person's achievement of a lifelong search for self-expression is another person's insanity. As much as we want to, it is important not to judge another's rituals. Common to all rituals is their significance to the participants and their value and power as a change agent. Rituals teach us who we are and what we strive to become.

When I created the exhibition using all my parents' clothing and textiles, I felt the need for a ritual. Discussing the idea with a Buddhist practitioner brought me to the idea of unmaking a quilt as a demonstration of the temporary nature of life. Buddhists create artworks called sand mandalas. They spend several days carefully arranging different-colored grains of sand into very intricate patterns. When they have completed the design, they blow it away, demonstrating life's impermanence. I varied the idea by using other people's objects that were associated with particular memories to create the piece. During the ritual, they would take back their objects, and that would be the unmaking of the piece. Because my parents were gone and I was now the head of the family, I called it my "wise woman" coming-of-age ceremony. I represented myself as a peacock, someone willing to stand up and show the wisdom of age. I enlisted all my friends from my various group connections to participate. At a private meeting several weeks preceding the ritual, each gave me her objects of memory. After receiving the materials, I asked each woman to write me a message on one of my mom's linen tablecloth napkins. I took each woman's collection of objects and made them into individual peacock feathers. I then attached these fabricated feathers to a coat made from the signed napkins.

The first person presented me with seemingly incongruous items: keys, greeting cards, ID cards, and balls of yarn. I sat with the items for a couple of weeks, fearing I was in over my head and it couldn't actually be completed. When I finally joined the disparate items, I found simple solutions that worked. I didn't have to use the whole ball of yarn but instead could use pieces of yarn to attach the keys. I could sew the greeting cards and the ID cards to the fabric. In the end, over forty women participated. The only similarity to each piece became its shape as that of a larger-than-life peacock feather, each with a loop and button at each end for attaching it to the coat.

Friendship Quilts

Friendship Quilts remind us of dear friends and beloved relatives. It is a way to demonstrate our love for each other through textiles. These quilts, filled with memories and emotions, can mark transitions. For example, a Friendship Quilt can be made for a friend who is moving to a distant place and who may never see those who signed it again. In past times, many a lonely woman living on an isolated homestead out West had only her Friendship Quilt as a cherished memory of the time when she lived among family and friends. Names on a quilt became precious remembrances of past loving relationships. Friendship Quilts served as a prized memory regardless of location. They were both for women who moved on and for those who stayed in one place.

Signature Quilts can be made from a single block pattern, called a Friendship Quilt, or made of different blocks, called a Sampler Album Quilt. Sampler Album Quilts are made up of several unique intricately pieced or appliquéd blocks. A friendship single pattern quilt is made by sewing a simple block pattern from available yard goods or fabric scraps. Signatures are written with indelible ink or they may be embroidered. Occasionally one person with beautiful handwriting inscribes all the signatures. Each quilt is special and unique, with the particular signatures of the friends and family who sign it.

Usually, each woman would make and sign her own block to be later sewn with other blocks into a Friendship Quilt. But there were other ways a Friendship Quilt could be created. Sometimes one person collected bits of fabric from others, made a block from each person's contribution, and then signed each block with that person's name. Many quilts included not only the names of women but of children and men as well. These quilts were made by sewing together readily available fabric or scraps of old clothing. The making of these quilts was within the reach of almost any woman no matter her financial circumstances and technical skill as a quilt maker.

Friendship Quilts took time. There was the process of collecting fabric or blocks from each person, piecing them, and then quilting the layers. Individual blocks on a quilt may be made over several years, and sometimes they were not made into a quilt until years later. No matter how they were made, they all had the same purpose—to record memories of cherished friends and family members.

Friendship Quilts are a way to stay connected with dear friends and relatives without the phone or the Internet. In our busy world, we must make a concerted effort to engage in the Friendship Quilt process. We can enlist a skilled friend to facilitate the process or maybe even make the actual quilt for us. People can sign their names on a piece of fabric before the quilter sews the blocks together. Or we can present a finished quilt at a special gathering such as a retirement party and have everyone sign a block on the quilt at that time. Any block pattern with a space for signatures is acceptable for a Friendship Quilt.

In our computerized world, quilted memories can take an exciting new turn. We can print actual photos of friends and family on fabric using our computer. If you don't have the equipment to do this, you can have it done at the many businesses offering copying services. Quilting and scrapbooking shops also offer this service, and in addition they can teach you the process. There are several books available on making photo-transfer quilts. Quilts incorporating precious photos are popular gifts for birthdays, anniversaries, graduations, and retirements. We can adapt the Friendship Quilt as we like to make a product that is pleasing and exciting for its recipient.

RAIL FENCE SIGNATURE TABLECLOTH

This pattern is from a signature quilt I made to celebrate my first one-woman show in 1987. I supplied precut blocks and pens at the opening reception and also throughout the length of the exhibit. People signed them, and after the show ended, I turned the blocks into a quilt. It is a 54-inch by 60-inch table topper.

You can gather your signatures at any point in the construction of the quilt. Because it's a tablecloth, we leave out the batting, making it more practical for a flat surface. When you gather your group together for an official ritual signing, include all the various elements of a ritual, such as candles, incense, wine, festive attire, and yummy refreshments, which will embellish the experience and give it a full depth of meaning.

The Rail Fence pattern is a simple one to make and has a great three-dimensional look when constructed with the right combination of light, medium, and dark fabrics.

Supplies

1½ yards of light cottons

1½ yards of medium cottons

1½ yards of dark cottons

½ yard for binding

2 yards 60-inch wide 100 percent cotton flannel

Sewing thread to match cotton flannel

Assorted permanent ink markers

Rail Fence pattern.

Directions

1. There are 56 6-inch rail blocks. Each rail is cut 2½ inches by 6½ inches . To cut the rails, cut 2½-inch strips across the width of the fabric, and then cut those into 6½-inch segments. Cut 56 of each light, medium, and dark value.

2. There are 34 6-inch border blocks. Each border block is cut 6½ inches by 6½ inches. To cut the

border blocks, cut 6½-inch strips the width of the fabrics, and then cut those into 6½-inch segments. Cut these randomly from the remnants of the fabrics.

3. Piece the rails into blocks, each block with a light on the left, a medium in the middle, and a dark on the right.

4. Piece the top into rows, keeping the large 6-inch border blocks at the outside edges.

5. Use the quilt-as-you-go method (see Introduction, p. 15) to sew the rows together and to the backing.

6. Trim the backing to match the patchwork and add a binding. (See Introduction, p. 15.)

7. Gather friends together to sign your quilt. Be sure to include your name, a date, and a blessing of your own.

Variations

- Gather the cotton shirts from family members and use these for the quilt top instead of yardage.

- Make and bring a signature quilt as a gift the next time you are invited to a birthday celebration.

- Start a signature quilt tradition for one of your family rituals (such as a birthday or holiday) that you can bring back each time the ritual is repeated.

- Instead of flannel, use a traditional batting and backing with hand quilting.

Conclusion

ARTFUL LIVING PIECE BY PIECE

Mitzrayim: *a narrow place; a personal enslavement.*

In the beginning when we were just getting to know each other, you sensed the compassion, touched the enthusiasm, and gleaned the scope of the work. You may have been slightly overwhelmed, wondering how this kind of spiritual practice might fit into your life. Now you not only know all my secrets, you have acquired a little stockpile of your own excitement, spirit, and cloth. Your life has been enriched with a mindful quilting practice that helps you in innumerable ways, shapes, and forms.

The core event in Judaism is the exodus from Egypt in the Hebrew Bible. Jews reenact the event every year at a home-based event called the Seder. The major idea is that we were *mitzrayim*, slaves in a narrow place, and now we are liberated beings in a wide open expanse.

On our quilting path we experience the same liberation. We affirm that life is here and now in our quilting and its ability to enable our journey. It is the vehicle for our continuing movement along our lifetime of efforts. Our quilts allow both the goal and the process in one magnificent creation after another. Our quilting generates the perfect combination of faith with action, hope with realism, and the universal with the particular, so that we are blissful and grateful in our co-creation experiences.

It's time to say goodbye, so how about creating a closing ritual? This one is yours. Keep it simple. It doesn't have to be big. How about inviting a friend for coffee and sharing something from this book? Or maybe do a silent meditation, asking a question about your quilting practice and guidance for the next step?

Another idea might be to buy and dedicate a new *Quilting Path* journal for the next phase of your growth. Or how about a night alone with your fabric—just cutting and piecing whatever occurs to you at that moment? Whatever your choice, go for it with all of you, and I promise vast lessons and enormous rewards. I will never leave you; I am always with you and I love you very much. Saying goodbye brings us one more opportunity for a refreshing hello.

Variations

Here are a few more ideas to help you continue on with your unique stitches:

- Plan a family retreat to make a Friendship Quilt.

- Form a *Quilting Path* support group of friends and neighbors.

- Revisit an individual attribute from the Tree of Life that needs more exploration. Reread the chapter and make one of the variations.

- Organize a field trip with friends to see a local quilt exhibition or go to a neighboring town's quilt shop.

- Take a skill-building quilting workshop.

- Spend an evening surfing the Net for quilting ideas.

- Have a fabric exchange party with your quilting friends.

SUGGESTED READING

Afterman, Allen. *Kabbalah and Consciousness*. Riverdale-on-Hudson, N.Y.: Sheep Meadow Press, 1992.

Albers, Josef. *Interaction of Color*. Rev. ed. New Haven: Yale University Press, 1975.

Beardsley, John, et al. *Gee's Bend: The Women and Their Quilts*. Atlanta: Tinwood Books, 2002.

Beck, Charlotte Joko. *Everyday Zen: Love and Work*. New York: HarperCollins, 1989.

Cameron, Julia. *The Artist's Way: A Spiritual Path to Higher Creativity*. New York: Jeremy P. Tarcher/Putnam, 1992.

Falk, Marcia. *The Song of Songs: A New Translation*. San Francisco: HarperSanFrancisco, 1990.

Frankiel, Tamar. *The Gift of Kabbalah: Discovering the Secrets of Heaven, Renewing Your Life on Earth*. Woodstock, Vt.: Jewish Lights Publishing, 2001.

Frankiel, Tamar. *Kabbalah: A Brief Introduction for Christians*. Woodstock, Vt.: Jewish Lights Publishing, 2006.

Kabat-Zinn, Jon. *Full Catastrophe Living: Using the Wisdom of Your Body and Mind to Face Stress, Pain, and Illness*. New York: Delta, 1990.

Kaplan, Rabbi Aryeh. *Inner Space: Introduction to Kabbalah, Meditation and Prophecy*. New York: Moznaim Publishing, 1990.

Kushner, Lawrence. *The Way into Jewish Mystical Tradition*. Woodstock, Vt.: Jewish Lights Publishing, 2001.

Lindbergh, Anne Morrow. *Gift from the Sea*. New York: Pantheon Books, 2005.

Lipsett, Linda Otto. *Elizabeth Roseberry Mitchel's Graveyard Quilt: An American Pioneer Saga*. Dayton, Ohio: Halstead & Meadows Publishing, 1995.

Matt, Daniel C., ed. *Zohar: Annotated & Explained*. Woodstock, Vt.: SkyLight Paths Publishing, 2002.

Quilt National 2005: The Best in Contemporary Quilts. Ashville, N.C.: Lark Publications, 2005.

Shapira, Kalonymus Kalman. *The Conscious Community: A Guide to Innerwork*. Northvale, N.J.: Jason Aronson, 1996.

Shulman, Jason. *Kabbalistic Healing: A Path to an Awakened Soul*. Rochester, Vt.: Inner Traditions, 2004.

Steinsaltz, Adin. *The Thirteen Petalled Rose*. New York: Basic Books, 1980.

Tishby, Isaiah, and Fischel Lachower. *The Wisdom of the Zohar: An Anthology of Texts*. 3 vols. The Littman Library of Jewish Civilization. New York: Oxford University Press, 1991.

ACKNOWLEDGMENTS

I am deeply grateful for and indebted to the loving people everywhere in my life: to my devoted family; to dearest Steve, cousin Ann Lee, and all of the Roots; to my study partner, Phyllis, and our meditation group; to my *Artist's Way* compatriots; to Jason and the Society of Souls; to Maura Shaw and the entire staff at SkyLight Paths Publishing; and to all of my old and new friends along the path. Thank you all.